EFFECTS OF JAPANESE INVESTMENT IN A SMALL AMERICAN COMMUNITY

A CASE STUDY OF AUTOPARTS IN EAST TENNESSEE

EFFECTS OF JAPANESE INVESTMENT IN A SMALL AMERICAN COMMUNITY

A CASE STUDY OF AUTOPARTS IN EAST TENNESSEE

SCOTT BRUNGER
YOUNG-BAE KIM
EDITORS

NOVA SCIENCE PUBLISHERS, INC.
Commack, NY

Creative Design: Gavin Aghamore
Editorial Production: Susan Boriotti
Assistant Vice President/Art Director: Maria Ester Hawrys
Office Manager: Annette Hellinger
Graphics: Frank Grucci
Acquisitions Editor: Tatiana Shohov
Book Production: Ludmila Kwartiroff, Christine Mathosian, Joanne Metal and Tammy Sauter
Circulation: Iyatunde Abdullah, Sharon Britton, and Cathy DeGregory

Library of Congress Cataloging-in-Publication Data
available upon request

ISBN 1-56072-454-4

6080 Jericho Turnpike, Suite 207
Commack, New York 11725
Tele. 516-499-3103 Fax 516-499-3146
E-Mail: Novascience@earthlink.net

Printed in the United States of America

CONTENTS

LIST OF TABLES AND FIGURES

PREFACE

This book began with a study sponsored by the Parker Fund for faculty development at Maryville College. The authors are grateful to the memory of Dr. Russell Parker, an inspiring teacher and a committed student of the social history of East Tennessee.

Both editors approach the study of Japanese investment in the East Tennessee from diverse backgrounds. Dr. Scott Brunger specializes in economic development, particularly in West Africa where he has done consulting work for voluntary organizations on aid projects. When he came to teach in East Tennessee in 1982, his interest in the economic development of this region during the past sixty years paralleled his concern for Africa. He began research on the impact of the Tennessee Valley Authority in raising the region from agrarian poverty to modern industry. His interest in Japanese investment is an outcome of his previous research.

The other editor, Dr. Young-Bae Kim, grew up in South Korea when it was a Japanese colony, so he learned Japanese in primary school. He also reads Chinese and Russian in order to pursue research on Russo-Japanese relationships as they affect the geo-politics of East Asia. He became interested in Japanese investment as a result of teaching a course in 1984 on Japanese management. Since then, the success of other East Asian economies and their penetration of the American market has broadened the emphasis of his course to East Asian management.

All the authors have visited or lived in Japan as well as worked in the United States. They bring to their studies a cross-cultural perspective in addition to their professional expertise.

The authors would like to dedicate this book to our families, who sacrificed to free us to do research. We like to thank Rachel Moore and Sheila Pirl for help on the manuscript and Nova Science Publishers for encouragement of this project.

We also thank many colleagues who have read and corrected our studies, though responsibility for the remaining errors remains with the editors.

Introduction

CROSS-CULTURAL PERSPECTIVE ON JAPANESE MANUFACTURING

Scott Brunger and Young-Bae Kim

Japanese manufacturing in the United States has elicited much speculation, some hopeful and some fearful. This book limits itself to one branch of Japanese manufacturing, auto parts, and one region, East Tennessee, in order to focus more closely. Emphasis on the region rather than the nation is appropriate. In the U.S. federal system, state and local governments recruit industry. A local community, which is seeking new jobs, has a different perspective on welcoming foreign investment than a nation seeking to conserve its auto production complex in Detroit.

The original contribution of the articles in this book is a cross-cultural perspective. Japanese management is not only changing American ways of working but also it is learning and being changed in the process. By focusing on the process of change and learning from experience this book will be helpful

(1) to foreign managers planning plants in the United States,
(2) to community leaders negotiating to bring in foreign plants,
(3) to opinion makers needing reassurance that both sides can learn from the strains of adjustment of foreign firms in American communities, and
(4) to scholars studying how the adjustments take place.

"Internationalization" and "globalization" have become important buzzwords in business as they reflect a changed mindset and government environment in which transnational firms operate. "Internationalization" implies that national boundaries no longer restrict market activities because transnational firms move products, capital, and expertise from nation to nation. In contrast to national markets, firms face a more complex international competitive environment and governments find that they have less influence over their national economy. Though "internationalization" is used as a neutral, technical word in most countries, its Japanese equivalent, *kokusaika*, developed a pejorative meaning during the mid-1980s, because it implied adaptation by the Japanese economy to pressures from the outside world. The Nakasone government had to cope with a huge trade surplus, which was recycled through overseas investments by Japanese banks and firms. Governments of the other advanced industrial nations pressured the Japanese government to take measures to open their financial markets and to raise their exchange rate making exports less competitive. These policy changes created new risks and new opportunities, including incentives to build Japanese automobiles overseas. However, the pressures were resented at home as a continuation of forced westernization that began with the U.S. occupation after World War II (Inoue). Because of its pejorative meaning "internationalization" will not be retained in this study.

"Globalization," transliterated as *gurobarization*, also recognizes a transnational firm's need to adapt to international competition but implies that different cultures require different forms of adaptation. This cross-cultural meaning of globalization has been promoted recently in the journal *Human Resources Management*, which organized forums from 1985 on. Professor Noel Tichy of the University of Michigan defines "globalization" as a "capacity to treat the world as one market while paradoxically dealing with it as many culturally diverse merchants" (Pucik, Tichy and Barnett, p.322). For Japanese companies globalization is especially challenging because their sources of competitive advantage in manufacturing have been closely tied to values in Japanese culture. In *Beyond National Borders: Reflections on Japan and the World*, a very successful book in its Japanese edition, Kenichi Ohmae of McKinsey and Company points out that Japanese firms in order to manufacture overseas would have to change staff training, personnel policies, communications in the head office, and accounting standards (42). Their corporate culture would have to open up to the rest of the world.

While "globalization" has become an important buzzword, practical experience in implementing globalization is less frequently recorded. The reason may well be that successes are proprietary information transferred internally within the global firm or through management consulting firms. Nevertheless, the need for global management training in business schools means that experiences with globalization need to be disseminated. By doing so, these chapters will be filling an important void.

In this book the first study, "Japanese Management Practices in an Autoparts Plant," shows how fundamental Japanese management practices have been adapted for American workers. In America recruitment sources no longer come from favored Japanese high schools and universities. Training has to be individually tailored because American workers lack a standardized background. Women also have a higher status in the U.S. workforce than in Japan, so the management must promote them just like men. Consensus management causes frustration for Americans who do not understand Japanese cultural nuances. Seniority promotion is not valued in American culture, nor is the commitment necessary for lifetime employment. The author worked in the plant for two years and experienced the stress of adapting Japanese management practices because she had to translate the arguments. She was put in the position of "bicultural communicator" as identified by Kenichi Ohmae, without the respect necessary to fulfill the role (p.104-5). In order to acquire the expertise necessary for her position, she enrolled in an MBA program at Tennessee Technological University.

The second study focuses on a specific problem of "Managing Reduction of Cumulative Trauma Injuries in a Joint Venture." Using the same machinery and work norms in plants in America and in Japan, the American workers suffered from repetitive motion disorders while the Japanese did not. Redesign of equipment, rotation of employees on each machine, more rigorous standardization of the work, and stretching exercises during breaks all help reduce the incidence of cumulative trauma. The firm instituted behavior based safety processes so that quality circles evaluate not only their production but also their work safety. However, differences remain between medical problems of American employees and those of employees in Japan operating the same equipment. These residual differences may be attributed to cultural attitudes toward work--where Japanese attempt to attain harmony with the machinery, Americans drive themselves to force the machinery and thus injure themselves. As human Relations Manager, the author has been intimately related to problems of worker safety since the design of the plant.

The third study is on the community environment for the Japanese autoplants. Based on a random survey of households, this study measures attitudes of a small American community toward Japanese investment. It finds higher socioeconomic attributes such as income, education, and foreign travel is positively related to acceptance of a Japanese firm. Age and female gender are negatively related to acceptance of a Japanese firm. Hope of finding a job at the firm is positively related to acceptance of a Japanese firm. Respondents have a more positive attitude toward foreign investment in their own community than toward foreign investment in the U.S., but they have a less positive attitude toward Japanese investment than foreign investment in general. Both authors teach at Maryville College, a Presbyterian liberal arts college with strong ties to Japan for the past century. The College helped bring the plant by offering English Language Studies and a Japanese Saturday School for children of employees.

The final study discusses "Culture Shock among Japanese Businessmen's Wives." The author, who taught English as a second language, developed a questionnaire which she administered to thirty-five wives of Japanese managers. She discovered that younger women adjust more easily but have more burdens of childcare so the stress in their lives is not comparable to that of older women. Culture shock among wives does not vary with time spent in the United States, as it does among Japanese students. Preparation before travel and English language studies diminish culture shock. The author concludes that culture shock is not prevalent among Japanese wives, partly because the company maintains a very structured hierarchy among wives as in Japan so in that sense the women never leave home. Today the author continues her interest in culture shock by working for a public relations firm in Tokyo that represents international companies.

Each study contains practical recommendations for Japanese firms operating in the United States. It also shows how experience gained in the United States applies to the company's global strategy.

JAPANESE MANUFACTURING IN US

Japanese manufacturing in the United States has elicited much speculation, some hope and some fear. One million workers are employed in the automobile industry in North America, making it the largest manufacturing sector. The wages earned by the million workers create local demand for goods and services that employ other workers in the locality. Conventional estimates are two local jobs for every auto job (Rubenstein, p.20, 230).

In 1994, 12.3 million motor vehicles were produced in the United States by all companies, compared to 10.6 million in Japan, 16.0 million in Europe, and 10.9 million in the rest of the world (*World Almanac 1996*, p.212). Japanese-owned auto assembly plants produced 30% of the world's automobiles in 1990 (Amoroso, p.457).

Within a Japanese automobile production system there is a hierarchy conferring advantages of better pay, better profits, and greater proportion of male workers at higher levels of assembly (Hill 466). Denso (called Nippondenso until 1996) is just below Toyota in the hierarchy (Toyota to Apply Japan Methods). Existing Tennessee companies are unlikely to subcontract for Denso, since to do so requires a high degree of dependency on production hierarchy, which only specialized firms would be likely to accept (Rubenstein, p.179).

Since the oil crisis of 1974 auto plants in the United States have clustered in the Midwest along interstate highways I-75 and I-65 as shown in the map below of "Locations of Japanese Auto Assembly Plants." In *The Changing US Auto Industry: A Geographical Analysis* James Rubenstein gives a persuasive reason that these plants cluster in the same region. Between the two interstate highways, Indiana is the geographical center of the automobile market. A single assembly plant will incur the lowest possible cost in shipping from that location to customers in the United States. Previous to the oil crisis U.S. automakers spread assembly plants along the coasts in order to diminish the cost of distributing assembled vehicles. They could do so because several plants produced each model of car. Automakers limited production to only three basic sizes of car-- compact, midsize and luxury. Several models of car could be built on an assembly line designed for a single size vehicle. Sales of multiple models within a region would be high enough to use efficiently the assembly line. Following the oil crisis competition forced automakers to add much smaller cars to their product mix. The increased variety of car sizes cannot be produced efficiently in assembly plants on the coast any longer. Each car size requires a separate assembly line, which has to supply the national market in order to achieve efficient scale. The necessity of producing for the national market as opposed to a regional market compels car companies to relocate assembly plants to the Midwest (pp.2-8, 137).

For the same reason Japanese automobile companies have also migrated to the Midwest. Honda built its assembly plant for motorcycles in 1978 followed by an auto plant two years later at Marysville, Ohio off I-75. Nissan came to Smyrna, Tennessee on I-65 in 1980. Mazda followed in 1985 by taking over an old Ford plant at Flat Rock, Michigan on I-75. Toyota built a plant at Georgetown, Kentucky on I-75. In 1986 Subaru and Isuzu located theirs in Lafayette, Indiana on I-65. Diamond Star joint venture of Chrysler and Mitsubishi built their plant in Normal, Illinois off I-65. Even the Canadian plants are located on the extensions of I-75: Suzuki in Ingersoll, Ontario, Toyota in Cambridge, Ontario, and Honda in Alliston, Ontario. (Rubenstein, p.6, 161, 209-13). The only exceptions are joint ventures: NUMMI (New United Motors Manufacturing, Inc.), Toyota's joint venture with General Motors in Fremont, California and the Ford/Mazda plant in

Hermosillo, Mexico. NUMMI gave Toyota experience manufacturing in the United States before committing to its own plant in Kentucky. The Ford/Mazda plant covers the Mexican market too. The map shows the locations of Japanese car assembly plants in the U.S. and Canada.

Japanese autoparts producers have also clustered on I-75 and I-65 near the assembly plants. The production principle of just-in-time delivery requires major component suppliers to locate close by in order to schedule deliveries by the hour. From 1985-90 Rubenstein counts 150 new Japanese autoparts companies, of which ten percent were located in Tennessee. The median distances from suppliers to assembly plants are 69 miles for Mazda, 150 miles for Honda, and 200 miles for Toyota (pp.171-173, 182). Short distances to assembly plants are especially important for scheduling deliveries by the hour, the practice at Japanese plants.

Some authors explain the concentration of Japanese auto assembly and autoparts plants in the Midwest as an orchestrated strategy. According to this view the Japanese Ministry of International Trade and Investment (MITI) picked the I-75 corridor south of Detroit in order to avoid the United Auto Workers (UAW) and to develop Japanese political support outside Michigan. This view assumes that state subsidies to attract autoplants are very significant in locational decisions, whereas Rubenstein finds transportation advantages limit choices to the Midwest anyway. It also assumes Mazda's location in Michigan as an aberration based on historic ties with Ford Motor Company and NUMMI's contract with the UAW as a result of re-opening a formerly unionized plant.

Furthermore, this view assumes that MITI has coordinating influence over Japanese auto producers. However, its influence over the smaller companies is restrained by their ties to U.S. automakers. Simon Reich, writing for the Georgetown University Institute for the Study of Diplomacy, finds that by 1979 MITI lost influence over the smaller Japanese automakers, Mitsubishi, Susuki and Mazda and Isuzu, as these sold stock to U.S. automakers in order to compete better with Nissan and Toyota (p.7). At the same time Nissan and Toyota are strong enough that they can determine their own investment strategies. While the imposition of "voluntary export restrictions" in 1981 on Japanese auto exports to the United States gave MITI the power to allocate 1.68 million vehicles among Japanese firms, construction of Japanese assembly plants soon eroded that power. On balance Rubenstein's view that geography determines locational decisions should be accepted.

Figure 1. Japanese car assembly plants in the US.

Even without central guidance by MITI, Japanese firms apparently achieve advantages by locating together in the same area. Successful implantation of a Japanese firm in an American community smooths the way for others to follow. The risk of rejection by officials and community leaders is lower when more have a stake in foreign investment. Experience with specialized Japanese services, such as translation, housing, and food supply, facilitates the coming of other firms. Efficiencies come from cultural agglomeration, just as efficiencies result from technical agglomeration of firms sharing expertise and skilled labor in a region.

As long as the foreign presence does not become so large as to provoke a backlash in the community, a strategy of follow-the-leader pays off. A community leader said he welcomed more Japanese firms until the golf courses get too crowded at tee-off time.

This strategy of cultural agglomeration works as well for German firms in the Spartanburg-Greenville area of South Carolina, across the mountains from East Tennessee. BMW built an assembly plant there. Mercedes-Benz produces vehicles in Vance, Alabama near I-65 and Volkswagen is coming to the South as well.

DISCUSSION OF JAPANESE MANUFACTURING TERMS

The implementation of Japanese manufacturing methods in America has brought with it a specialized vocabulary drawn from Japanese. This specialized vocabulary has English equivalents. Indeed many ideas were borrowed and improved upon. It may be argued that Japanese management developed out of traditional Japanese group decision-making combined with American statistical quality control techniques introduced by Edward Deming. The use of Japanese terms has been retained in America, because the goal is to change traditional manufacturing practices. The mindset conveyed by Japanese manufacturing terms helps desired changes occur.

This discussion serves to introduce the following terms that will be used in later chapters:

1) "Just-in-time production" or *kanban* is one way of keeping manufacturing costs down by avoiding large inventories of parts and supplies needed for the manufacture of a given product. In addition to low costs, it makes the maintenance of quality control easier since defective parts can be more quickly identified (Abegglen, Chap.5).

The creator of the Toyota production system was inspired by the organization of American supermarkets in which the act of re-stocking the shelves is accompanied by placing new orders. In the same way in the factory, as parts move on to the assembly line, *kanban* order cards from the parts container are sent back to suppliers to replace the parts. Order cards are then reduced until production occurs with a minimum of inventory.

"Just-in-time production" has the geographical effect of forcing suppliers of major auto components to locate within 200 miles of the vehicle assembly plant in order to deliver new orders within four hours. Since East Tennessee is less than 200 miles from Toyota, BMW, Saturn and Nissan, it becomes a favored location for autoparts plants.

2) Another way to streamline manufacturing is through "production leveling" or *heijunka. Heijunka* involves redesigning the production process to permit quick changeovers. In this way production runs of the each part can be shortened. The advantages are that parts are handled less from one stage of production to the next and, if defects are discovered at a later stage, fewer parts have to be scrapped. Waste or *muda* is reduced to a minimum.

A necessary result of production leveling is that workers must know several jobs to continue production after changeovers. Worker flexibility means fewer job categories for workers than are found in traditional American assembly lines and different labor relations. Japanese auto companies have a tradition in Japan of working with unions that are very cooperative by American standards. As a result, Japanese management has sought to locate in states with weak union traditions, such as Tennessee and other states in the South, or to renegotiate work rules with the United Auto Workers when taking over plants with unions, such as the Toyota-GM joint venture NUMMI in California and Mazda in Michigan (Parker, pp.28-29).

3) "Constant improvement" or *kaizen* is an obligation both of management and workers. While management's responsibility has been well known since Frederick Taylor introduced scientific management at the turn of the century, workers' responsibility has been a more elusive goal. Japanese firms provide in-depth training both in a variety of job skills but also in-group decision-making for production teams. Each production team has a meeting place near its workplace, where it can study quality control statistics and propose solutions to work problems. During work the *andon* board is lit over the assembly line. If work is on schedule, the light is green. If an operator is falling behind, the light is yellow. If a problem occurs that requires stopping the line, the light is red. Constant improvement or reduction of the work time at each station, the *takt* time, requires that the line move fast enough so that some of the lights are yellow (Parker, p.16).

The workers have responsibility to stop their assembly line, if they see defective parts coming to them. The line-stop principle or *jidoka* places product quality in the hands of the workers. In addition, an inspection display shows off the first part completed on the shift, the last part, and a random part in between. The displayed parts can be checked to see if tolerances change or work slackened during the course of the shift.

4) In contrast to Japanese production processes, which emphasize speed, their decision-making process is slow by American standards because it requires consensus throughout the group. *Nemawashi* means in Japanese "preparing the ground" prior to the transplanting of a tree to avoid damage to any roots. The "*nemawashi*" procedure is applied to the preparation of all elements of the company for a major decision. That is, once people who are likely to be affected by the decision are identified, they will be methodically consulted so that they commit themselves to support the proposal (Zimmerman, pp.124-25).

After the ground is prepared, the formal procedure for taking the decision is the *ringi* system. A document summarizing the decision is circulated and signed or stamped with a seal *ringi* by all those who have read the document. Although the *nemawashi* process may have involved debate on the options for the group, the *ringi* document demonstrates that the decision was made by consensus.

The above principles of Japanese management will be referred to in the studies that follow.

East Tennessee Communities

This study focuses on an American community where the cross-cultural effects of Japanese investment can be observed. Since the advent of the Nissan assembly plant in Smyrna and the Saturn plant in Spring Hill, Tennessee has become a source of motor vehicles. Located next to I-65 in Middle Tennessee, the two plants together assemble 600,000 units a year and provide 14,000 jobs. Supplying them are four hundred autoparts plants employing a total of 64,000 Tennesseans (Martin, p.1E).

The map "Japan's Investment in Tennessee" shows the location of all cities where Japanese-owned businesses are located. Those cities where no Japanese-owned businesses are linked to the auto industry have been crossed out. On the right all of the East Tennessee cities have auto-related plants, except Athens and Lenoir City. Only three towns in Middle Tennessee and two in West Tennessee have no Japanese investments related to the motor vehicle industry.

Figure 2. Japanese investment in Tennessee.

As an isolated semi-rural community, Blount County represents an ideal laboratory for studying the impact of foreign-owned industry in the United States. Blount County is located in the Tennessee Valley, fifteen miles south of Knoxville. Culturally it is part of Appalachia, so it has a history of out-migration to work in northern factories. Large-scale manufacturing began in the 1920s when the Aluminum Company of America (ALCOA), based in Pittsburgh, built its first aluminum plant in a company town, Alcoa, Tennessee. Then in 1933 the Tennessee Valley Authority with its main offices in Knoxville began building the electric power generation facilities that attracted more heavy industry. Today the county is known for manufacturing fiberglass boats, textiles and rubber products as well as aluminum. Its major service industries are an international quality control consulting firm, Maryville College, a Presbyterian liberal arts school founded in 1819, and tourism in the Great Smoky Mountains National Park.

In the 1990 population census, Blount County had a population of 85,969. In 1987 according to *County Business Patterns 1988*, 21,156 employees worked in manufacturing earning an annual payroll of $374 million. The median household income was $30,300 in 1994 (*County and City Data Book 1994*).

Blount County is accessible to Interstate 40, which connects North Carolina to California, and Interstate 75, which runs from Michigan to Florida. Delivery times to the Toyota plant in Georgetown, Kentucky and to the Nissan plant in Smyrna, Tennessee are less than four hours so deliveries can be made on the just-in-time system.

Two Japanese autoparts companies recently located here, Denso and Toyota Tsusho. A Japanese producer of medical lasers also recently arrived, as did a Canadian firm. Three British firms producing coal conveyors, tire drums, and lumber have been present so long that local citizens forget they are foreign too.

Many factors make East Tennessee a desirable location for Japanese manufacturing. The region is located Interstate 75. The workforce is compliant to new production methods, so Japanese manufacturing techniques can be introduced. The latitude is similar to Tokyo, which makes the weather desirable for Japanese managers. State political leadership actively courted Japanese investment.

Denso is a Japanese company closely allied with Toyota. It began negotiations in Blount County in 1987 to build three plants for manufacturing alternator/starters, instrument clusters and air conditioning amplifiers. The first two began production in summer 1990 and the last in 1992. The plants sell to most Japanese manufacturers in the U.S. as well as to Chrysler, Ford and General Motors. They hired four hundred workers as of June 1990 with a planned eventual workforce above one thousand. The anticipated increase in aggregate personal income in the community would be $17 million and an additional 563 non-manufacturing jobs. The plants are predicted to generate $1 million in tax revenues for the county and $800,000 for the city (Butler). Denso's total investment will come to $255 million. Currently it employs 1,800 Americans and 90 Japanese.

The American employees hired at Denso represent about 4.6% of the working population of the county or 4.5% of the manufacturing workers who are in the upper echelon in pay as well. The 150 Japanese engineers and managers hired to start operations at the plant represent an identifiable, if temporary, new source of demand. This market induces supermarkets to stock new foods, video stores to rent samurai movies, restaurants to alter menus, and builders to remodel homes (Rubenstein, p.293).

REFERENCES

Abegglen, James and George Start Jr. *Kaisha: The Japanese Corporation* New York: Basic Books, 1984.

Amoroso, B. "Economic Globalization: Labour Options and Business Strategies in High Labour Cost Countries" *Columbia Journal of World Business* 1992.

Hill, Richard Child "Comparing Transnational Production Systems: The Automobile Industry in the USA and Japan" *International Journal of Urban and Regional Research* Fall 1990, pp.462-480.

Inoue, Shosos "Review of The Challenge of Japan's Internationalization: Organization and Culture" *Japan Quarterly* 31(4) pp.462-464, 1988.

Kawata, Makoto "Making it Work: Japanese Direct Investment in the United States" *Journal of Japanese Trade & Industry* No.1, 1984, pp.25-27.

Martin, Tim "A Win for the South" *The Tennessean--Nashville* September 30, pp.1E,5E.

Ohmae, Kenichi *Beyond National Borders: Reflections on Japan and the World* Homewood, IL: Dow Jones-Irwin, 1987.

Parker, Mike and Jane Slaughter *Choosing Sides: Unions and the Team Concept* Boston: A Labor Notes Book, South End Press, 1988.

Pucik, Vladamir, Noel Tichy and Carole Barnett, "Globalizing Management: Creating and Leading the Competitive Organization" New York: John Wiley & Sons, 1992.

Reich, Simon *Restraining Trade to Invoke Investment: MITI and the Japanese Auto Producers* Washington, D.C.: Georgetown University Institute for the

Study of Diplomacy, Pew Case Studies in International Affairs, Case 150, part A.

Rubenstein, James M. *The Changing US Auto Industry: A Geographical Analysis* New York: Routledge, Chapman and Hall, Inc. 1992.

"Toyota to Apply Japan Methods to Parts Procurement in U.S. "*The Japan Economic Journal*, March 21, 1987, p.20.

U.S. Department of Commerce, Bureau of Census *County and City Data Book 1994.*

_______ *Population Census 1990.*

The World Almanac 1996 Mahwah, N.J.: Funk & Wagnalls Corp.

Zimmerman, Mark *How to do Business with the Japanese* New York: Random House, 1985.

Chapter 1

JAPANESE MANAGEMENT PRACTICES IN AN AUTOPARTS PLANT

Noriko Chapman

Like other large multinational enterprises, Japanese companies are discovering that they must adapt to the local culture wherever they operate. Internationalization, where companies operate identical divisions overseas, is no longer sufficient. Globalization is becoming more popular and important as managers and workers in a company adjust their worldwide business to different cultures (Ohmae).

According to Peters, a company needs people who are aware of changes and have skills to adjust to different cultures. Many Japanese companies are going abroad. People from all over the world are coming to Japan. Young Japanese are being westernized. Japanese management style needs to change to adjust to these changes.

Four Japanese personnel management traditions need review before being used overseas: recruitment and training, consensus management, seniority promotion and lifetime employment. The following section will discuss their relevance in the United States.

First, many Japanese companies use a unique system of hiring employees through close relationships with universities and high schools. Japanese society emphasizes which school a person graduated from rather than what kind of skills or education the person received. The special relationships between particular companies and universities keep harmony in the company since it hires managers from the same background as the senior executives. The way of hiring employees also keeps a company conservative.

Recently to compensate for this problem, some Japanese companies announced that they would hire on the basis of interviews without requiring job candidates to submit their resumes. The companies wanted to find outstanding employees who were not satisfied with prestige from diplomas but wanted to work according to their ability.

A company spends much time and money on its training program, such as on-the-job training. In many cases, the training is based on the company ideology. It takes time and money for a company to train employees. As a result, it is hard for the company to respond to rapid change because the employees need retraining.

Secondly, consensus management slows down a company's ability to respond to change. The *ringi* system is a unique way to implement consensus management in many Japanese companies. *Ringi* means that a formal proposal is passed around among managers who have the opportunities to register their agreement by their seals. The number of seals can range from five to twelve. That is, five to twelve managers help make a decision. Furthermore, to complete the *ringi* system successfully, *nemawashi* is necessary. *Nemawashi* is an informal discussion before the *ringi* document is presented (Sethi, p.34). Literally, *nemawashi* means digging around the roots of the tree without killing the tree. Informal consultations avoid conflicts when the formal decision is presented. But then, the *ringi* system is a redundant decision-making step, since the decision is almost always made during the *nemawashi* stage. *Ringi* slowly formalizes the consensus without making a better decision (Yang, p.173).

Thirdly, the seniority promotion system is one of the practices which slows down company functions. Following recruitment at an educational level, the number of years spent in the company determines the level of remuneration. This practice is believed to prevent employees from competing for their promotion and to achieve harmony in an organization where the employees recognize that they are working for the whole business. However, since the shortage of senior posts has become a serious problem in many big Japanese companies, young managers compete harder to attain the senior posts. The current seniority promotion system shows young employees that they have fewer opportunities for promotion because even their bosses have a hard time climbing the ladder (Mroczkowski and Hanaoka, p.40). Japanese executives advance based on their ability to negotiate within the company rather than outside (Yang, p.180).

Lifetime employment is a significant difference between American management styles and Japanese management styles. A Japanese worker enters a company soon after his/her graduation from university or high school and works for the company until retirement at 57 to 60 years old. Lifetime employment creates employee stability and a high degree of employee loyalty. On the other hand, this practice lets many Japanese managers be lazy because job security is guaranteed without hard work. Furthermore, there are senior employees called *madogiwa-zoku*, meaning "employees who sit beside windows." They have been put on the sidelines and must bear boredom and indignity in exchange for job security (Yang, p.180).

Lifetime employment reflects Japanese society significantly, although only about a third of the working population benefit from it (Sethi, p.vi). Many Japanese people feel secure by belonging to a larger organization. Therefore, this practice is the most difficult change that could be attempted by a company. Japanese companies do not want to hire employees who have worked for several companies, although to do so would bring in new expertise.

APPLICATION OF JAPANESE MANAGEMENT IN EAST TENNESSEE

Given the above Japanese management practices how can they be adapted to a different culture in the United States? For two years I worked with a Japanese autoparts company as a translator. My job was mainly translating oral conversations for both Japanese and American employees. To start with, I worked in the training center where new employees develop a certain level of skills on grinding, drilling, and filing machines. I also translated written materials from Japan, such as instructions for maintenance, parts production, and quality control.

Recruitment and Training

American recruits arrive with various working experiences, unlike Japanese recruits with homogeneous backgrounds. The result is that training programs in Tennessee must be tailored to individual abilities and deficiencies. In the beginning Japanese trainers gave lectures and the same exercises to all trainees, but they adapted and let American trainees read a textbook and do some exercises to demonstrate mastery of skills.

Many American trainees seem to feel uncomfortable taking courses without a clear explanation of the importance for their job assignments of the training. Some training requires American trainees to improve their basic skills. Japanese trainers believe that basic skills are necessary to improve employee's skills for their future jobs. Attitudes differ toward training because Japanese look at education as a high value in itself, while Americans have a more pragmatic attitude that education should do things for them.

Japanese companies in the United States must be careful to hire women of equal qualifications along with men. Japanese women have traditionally been discriminated against by male workers. However, under Japan's Equal Employment Opportunity Law which was legislated in 1986, many large companies started hiring female college graduates as full-time workers. Up until then only 23% of women found jobs upon graduation versus 77% of the men (Lansing and Ready, p.115). Traditionally, Japanese culture expects women to quit working outside after marriage. Because of women's short work life, many Japanese companies do not want to hire women under the same conditions as male workers. Since American women have more experience in the workforce, they can help conservative Japanese managers to become progressive in terms of their culture.

In Japan recruiters want employees to be loyal to the company and their team (Alston, p.237). This loyalty permits the company even to send them without their families to work in the United States.

Consensus Management

Japanese bottom-up decision making depends on everyone desiring consensus. However, there is a question of how many Americans can understand the need for consensus. One need is to improve American employee's skills in making decisions in a group. American workers cannot understand that the Japanese are doing their jobs horizontally through consultation with others at the same level rather than moving information up and down the chain of command.

The consensus system in Japan also has some tricks that may escape American employees. In *nemawashi*, the informal discussion preceding a decision, the boss implies to his subordinates what he wants and then lets them come up with the proposal based on the manager's intention. In other words, subordinates have the opportunity to manipulate the boss' ideas.

This process seems impractical to American employees. For example, in the maintenance department both Japanese and American managers were supposed to attend a meeting with executives and present some ideas about training the workers. The Japanese manager asked the American manager if he had any ideas. The American responded that even if he had a good idea, it would be rejected if it challenged established practices. In short, he was given a chance to propose but without much chance of acceptance.

Another possible strategy for developing consensus is called *matomari*, similar to running an idea up the flagpole to see if anyone salutes. The executive presents a general proposal without detailed feasibility studies. If the American manager in maintenance had realized the possibility exists for brainstorming his idea, he might have been able to contribute. Instead, he was afraid that the Japanese manager would not accept it unless detailed plans were made.

In any type of discussion, a Japanese manager takes a lot of time to come to a point, which seems to frustrate American employees. Many Japanese do not indicate what they are talking about at the beginning of their speech. Moreover, many Japanese do not say either "Yes" or "No" directly. Japanese listeners can determine from the context the approval or disapproval without a direct "Yes" or "No." From my experience, I always had a hard time translating synonyms for "Yes" and "No," which have several different meanings in the sentences depending upon which situations they refer to. The meanings can be:

- "Yes, I agree with the idea but do not take an action yet"
- "I am not sure about the issue, so please let me have some time to think about it" or
- "No, I do not agree with the idea, but I do not want to reject it now because of the person's feelings."

The reason that these responses are ambiguous is that Japanese do not want to be seen as too aggressive or individualistic (Alston, p.345). However, since American culture is aggressive and individualistic, the listener expects a clear response rather than one designed to maintain consensus.

Informal methods of consensus building would be easier to work out without language barriers. As long as the factory in America requires many Japanese for maintenance and training, two separate networks of communication co-exist. It is hard to pass information between them.

Many differences between American and Japanese employees could be solved by consensus building. If they were aware of the differences between each other, they would discuss them, make compromises and determine the best practices in the new situation. However, there is a problem that not many American and Japanese employees realize what the differences are. Often, the translator must ask both sides to clarify their position for the other.

Seniority Promotion and Lifetime Employment

Because Japanese employees plan to spend their careers working for one company, they think of themselves as part of a company family. The president of the auto-parts firm expects American employees to be part of the company family too (Taira, 1990, p.2). American employees say that they feel relief that they will not be laid off or fired. They also appreciate how patient the Japanese workers are in teaching them. The difficulty comes with from the personality adjustments necessary for lifetime employment.

In Tennessee it is difficult for the company to expect all American employees to have loyalty to the company because many of them are not familiar with lifetime employment. When I visited the factory in Japan, workers can explain not only their job but also the products that the company produced and the training programs. American workers with less personal investment in the company do not know about the rest of the organization.

Lifetime employment also results in different attitudes towards working overtime. Many Japanese workers do not object to staying late at their workplaces, not only in Japan but also in the United States. Japanese workers tend to stay late at their work places to avoid being disloyal to those still working (Alston, p.157). During the start up period in Tennessee many team leaders needed to complete paper work such as planning on-the-job training for their associates. One day an American team leader complained about too much paperwork because he wanted to emphasize hands-on work. However, the Japanese manager suggested that he do the paperwork after quitting time. The team leader answered "No" because overtime work is for emergencies, not for paperwork.

The same system of seniority promotion which is practiced in Japan cannot be successful in the United States. If the Japanese company attempts to use it, the company would lose enthusiastic American employees but keep unimaginative ones. If more pay is guaranteed according to length of service, there might be employees who are just at work places without working hard for eight hours a day. The seniority system in Japan is embedded within a culture that respects age (Cole, p.3). Therefore, it seems unfair to American employees who emphasize their abilities and skills.

There was a good example demonstrating American employee's frustration about being paid differently based on length of service in the same position. At the autoparts company, there are three ranks of associates based on length of experience in their own field: the highest are A-ranked, then B-ranked, and finally the newest are C-ranked. The employees work side-by-side in each department.

One B-ranked associate complained about being paid less than an A-ranked one although he performed almost the same job. Furthermore, he could not understand the apprenticeship system which required a certain period of training and then required employees to rise to the upper rank based on time in service. I interviewed a Japanese personnel manager and he explained that he understood the differences between Japanese workers and American workers but that they had not yet instituted a well organized wage system (August, 1990).

Some of the management practices are based on lifetime employment, e.g. open-door policy, management by walking around and quality circles. The open-door policy helps employees recognize that they are working together rather on than on their own projects. In a large office without walls the department head can keep an eye on the workflow. Open offices also strengthen group loyalty and worker-to-worker cooperation because communication is face-to-face (Alston, p.163). Employees also feel more comfortable about communicating with their boss without entering a separate office (*Zaibei*, 1989 p.33).

Management by walking around is practiced at the autoparts firm. The president sets the tone by visiting employees in their place of work and holding conversations with them on the job. He stays informed about work and the employees have a line of communication with the top manager.

Quality circles require good communication between employees based on the understanding that constant improvement in work will not result in job loss. Their success requires two-way communication between Japanese and American workers so that each can learn from the other's experience. Quality circles fit in with a training system that provides flexible skills so that as work is redesigned the employees can adapt to new ways.

PROPOSALS FOR ADAPTING JAPANESE PERSONNEL MANAGEMENT

(1) While it is important that Japanese management needs to be flexible for Americans, it is also crucial that American employees are flexible adapting Japanese management practices. Even if American workers acquire the habit of group work, they are not totally cooperative but competitive. For Americans pay should not be based on seniority but based on work done. The Japanese practice of comprehensive worker training should be maintained because it offers greater work flexibility and opportunity to improve technology. Since all workers master similar

skills and jobs are vaguely defined, there will be smaller wage differences than in American style plants (Alston, p.235).

(2) Good communication among workers must be stressed in order to overcome the language barrier. The Japanese need to listen to Americans very carefully and should ask the Americans to repeat until they understand each other. Unless the Japanese know exactly what the Americans mean, there will be trouble emerging sooner or later on the job. In addition, Japanese need to give good reasons for their work practices. Even when some Japanese ways have been successful in Japan, they may be strange and impractical for Americans. If Japanese explain their methods and Americans understand what they expect, the Japanese should let the Americans try it first so they can watch the method. After Americans try the Japanese way, both need to discuss the results. Americans might have better ideas to improve the process. Some job frustration would be reduced through more careful communication on both sides.

(3) During break time and meals, the Japanese should not separate themselves from Americans. Even though communication is difficult across the language barrier, the sense of confidence and understanding brought through informal meeting will boost teamwork on the job.

Japanese companies are aware of these difficulties. The president of the company stated in a newspaper interview, "The inability to communicate in English has been the most difficult transition in moving to Blount County" (*The Daily Times*, p.3D). Hopefully many Japanese companies in the United States can overcome this difficulty and truly globalize their operations.

References

Alston, J.P (1986). *The American Samurai: Blending American and Japanese Managerial Practices* Berlin; New York: de Gruyter.

Brown, R.M., & Blevins, T.F. (1989). Should America embrace Japanese management techniques? *SAM Advanced Management Journal*, *54*(1), 22-31.

Cole, R.E. & Deskins, D.R.jr. (1988). Racial factors in site location and employment patterns of Japanese auto firms in America. *California Management Review*, *31*(1), 9-12.

The Daily Times. (October 17, 1990). 3D.

Lansing, R., & Ready, K. (1988) Hiring women managers in Japan: An Alternative for Foreign Employers. *California Management Review, 30*(3), 112-127.

Mcroczkowski, T., & Hanaoka, M. (1989). Continuity and change in Japanese management. *California Management Review, 31*(2), 39-53.

Ohmae, K. (1987). *Beyond National Borders*. Tokyo: Kodansha.

Peters, T.J. (1989). (Interviewee). *Super Seminar* (Program #1). Tokyo: NHK.

Sethi, S.P. (1984). *The false promise of the Japanese miracle: Illusions and realities of the Japanese management system*. Boston: Pitman.

Taira, M. (1990). *NDTN. 1*(1) Nippondenso Tennessee, Inc.

Yang, C.Y. (1984). Demystifying Japanese management practices. *Harvard Business Review, 62*, 172-182.

Zaibei nikkei sezougyou no kadai to taiou-- Survey of Japanese manufacturing companies in the U.S. (1989). New York: Keizai Dantai Rengokai.

Chapter 2

Managing Reduction of Cumulative Trauma Injuries in a Joint Venture

Larry Thomas

Background

In 1989 a joint venture was formed between a leading Japanese and American auto parts maker to produce steering assemblies in East Tennessee. From the Japanese, the joint venture adapted the production system used by Toyota. From the Americans, it developed an American-managed, team-based participative management system. The results achieved by blending the best of both systems surpassed expectations. Except for one unforeseen complication, the joint venture exceeded its lofty goals for quality, market share, and pricing strategies. What they did not expect was the tremendous number of cumulative trauma injuries that began in late 1991.

Figure 3 gives the cases of cumulative trauma for the first four years of operations. As production levels increased on new assembly lines in 1990 and 1991, the number of cumulative trauma incidents rose to levels unacceptable to the company, yet they rose higher in 1992. Identification of the cause of cumulative trauma and its abatement became an increasing concern. The joint venture production technicians may be their own worst enemy. In Japan the mother-corporation does not have a cumulative trauma problem, while the joint venture does. Yet the production techniques are virtually identical. The joint venture's management team, ergonomic committee, and their Workman's

Compensation Insurance carrier now believe attitude and behaviors are more of a contributing factor than originally thought. The joint venture based current safety and health efforts on these beliefs.

Figure 3. Cumulative Trauma Cases.

This paper will describe the joint venture efforts to manage its cumulative trauma problem. The first part will describe the production philosophy and team-based participative management system. It will also define cumulative trauma, and the occupational risk factors that cause it. The chronology section will review the cumulative trauma incident rates, the past efforts to correct the problems, and the results of these efforts. Finally, recommendations will review current plans, anticipated results, and why the joint venture believes these plans will be effective.

A Japanese named Taiichi Ohno developed The Toyota Production System. On a trip to the United States in 1956, the way in which American supermarkets operated impressed Ohno. Their methods of supply and distribution enabled customers to buy what they wanted, when they wanted, with little wasted time or materials. A detailed, comprehensive system eventually evolved at Toyota. Not only is it difficult for American manufacturers to learn and mimic this system, it is extremely difficult for American workers to adjust to the rigorous physical and mental demands this system imposes on them.

The Joint Venture Production System

The joint venture initially adopted the Toyota Production System, complete with all its Japanese terminology. The machining lines and assembly lines incorporated the principles of *jidoka* and *heijunka*. Instead of huge, automated, mass production machines that took days to retool or fix if broken, the joint venture installed simple, computer-controlled machines that only performed one or two functions. Instead of automatically transferring parts from one machine to another, a production technician will load, unload, and transfer the parts from machine to machine. At each machine, there is a quality check on the part, performed by the technician just before loading.

Each line established *takt* times, and then carefully balanced the line to these times. The *takt* times started at 60 seconds, but *kaizen* activities brought the time down to 45 seconds on the newer lines. *Takt* time is an integral part of work cell arrangement. Production technicians continuously walk the loops, unloading, inspecting, and loading anywhere from 4 to 8 machines in the designated takt time (45 to 60 seconds).

The joint venture uses a *kanban* system of material flow. Parts to the various lines are delivered in small quantities, just in time for the line's production needs. Although this system is excellent for tracking materials, controlling inventory, and cutting costs, it keeps technicians constantly working to maintain each line's production needs.

Each loop has its work standardized. Each technician working a loop must perform tasks according to the standardized work instructions for that loop. The instructions include many details. They include instructions on how to hold the part, how to position the wrist and arm, and which hand to use.

In 1991, the joint venture created a training program based on the Toyota model. Its goal was to produce using less human effort, less inventory, less time, and higher quality. The process described in the preceding paragraphs accomplishes all of that except for one very important item--"less human effort."

In one respect, the joint venture system does use less human effort. It runs at minimum manning levels, but the employees working in this system are in constant motion and work harder than their counterparts at more traditional plants. The joint venture production technicians are constantly walking a loop totaling up to seven miles a day of actual walking. Each loop contains a wide variety of tasks. *Kaizen*, the continual search for improvement, has eliminated most wasteful motions. The Japanese consider any waste (including wasted time) *muda* and constantly strive to eliminate it. The net effect is faster *takt* times with the same number of people. This equates to more movement (work) per person, per given unit of time. The rapidity of movement and the lack of slack (rest) times are two of the contributing factors to the joint venture cumulative trauma problems.

This issue is not unique to the joint venture. Joseph and Suzy Fucini describe Mazda's experience in *Working for The Japanese.* Mazda built a plant in Flat Rock, Michigan to produce cars. Mazda completed a contract with the United Auto Worker's union (UAW) that allowed the Japanese to implement a production system modeled after the Toyota Production System. This is very similar to the system implemented at the joint venture. Mazda has its ergonomic problems highlighted in the chapter on Safety and Health. The chapter compares the cumulative trauma rate at Flat Rock to the "Big Three" American automobile manufacturers. Flat Rock's rate is much higher. This is attributed to employees at Flat Rock working 57 seconds out of each minute. This compares to 45 seconds per minute in the "Big Three" (p.180).

As one can see, the apparent reasons for cumulative trauma at Mazda, are very similar to the joint venture. The question still remains, why do the Japanese not have similar problems in identical production facilities in Japan? Part of the problem (or solution) may lie in the team-based management system implemented at the joint venture.

The Team-Based Participative Management System

One of the first major decisions made during the creation of the joint venture was to make employee involvement a way of life. The joint venture hired a Human Relations Manager with a strong background in team systems. His booklet *Preliminary Selection and Training Plan*, describes the original technician hiring process, training, and his first attempt at defining the future team system at the joint venture.

The goal of each team is to become self-reliant on its own members to operate, maintain and improve their area of business. A good team has open, honest, and frank problem solving relationships among its members. They look for ways to support and learn from one another and their management resources to continually improve the effectiveness of their business area.

In order to accomplish its goals, a team must:

1. Be responsible for a given work area on a particular shift.
2. Consist of a stable group who work together.

3. Become self-reliant in developing the skills to operate, maintain and improve its work area,
4. Consist of 5 to 15 members.
5. Operate its part of the business in a responsible and effective manner.
6. Help develop and keep each individual team member's attitude, performance and conduct up to high standards.
7. Operate on a basis of joint ownership and responsibility for the total task, without separate ownership by any one member; it's not up to just one person by himself.
8. Have members who are responsible to train one another and develop one another in technical and problem solving skills.
9. Have members who are responsible for inventing and carrying out better ways of running their part of the business.
10. Firmly believe in consistently trying to adhere to the joint venture values.

(Thomas, 1988, p. 45).

Added to the basic concepts listed above were a set of ten responsibilities. These responsibilities included safety, quality, productivity improvement, planning, general business, goal setting, communications, pay qualifications, labor utilization, hiring process, and discipline. In traditional systems, these responsibilities belong to first line supervision. At the joint venture they were to belong to the teams and their team leader coordinators.

The team coordinator's role is detailed with thirteen specific responsibilities that range from coordinating work flow, record keeping, facilitating meeting, etc., to actual hands-on work when time allows. The role of the Team Coordinator is to aid the team in achieving three primary goals:

1. To acquire the skills necessary to perform effectively.
2. Channel the effort of individuals as a team to achieve organizational and team objectives.
3. Aid the team members in developing and exercising self management capabilities (p. 49).

The joint venture incorporated most of the original concepts into its current team system. The team coordinator became a team leader, but the responsibilities remained the same. The joint venture adopted the basic concepts of the business unit teams with minor modifications to the makeup.

The team system at the joint venture is a two-edged sword. Production, quality, and other measurable goals consistently beat expectations. The joint venture is now profitable, over one year earlier than predicted in the strategic plan. The other side of the sword is "stress," an enormous amount of it.

The teams have accepted a wide range of responsibilities. With the responsibility comes accountability. With accountability comes pressure to perform. With pressure comes stress, a tremendous amount. This stress may be one of the contributing factors to the cumulative trauma problem at the joint venture.

Cumulative Trauma

The Occupational Safety and Health Administration (OSHA) has created a draft standard for ergonomics called *Ergonomics Program Management Recommendations for General Industry*. OSHA defines cumulative trauma disorders as:

> . . . the term used for health disorders arising from repeated biomechanical stress due to ergonomic hazards. . . CTDs [cumulative trauma disorders] are a class of musculoskeletal disorders involving damage to the tendons, tendon sheaths, synovial lubrication to the sheaths, and the related bones, muscles, and nerves of the hands, wrists, elbows, shoulders, neck, and back. The more frequently occurring occupationally induced disorders in this class include carpal tunnel syndrome, epicondylitis (tennis elbow), tendonitis, tenosynovitis, synovitis, stenosing tenosynovitis of the finger, DeQuervain's disease, and low back pain (1990, glossary).

The joint venture has experienced a wide range of cumulative trauma disorders (CTDs). Although there are many different forms of CTDs, all can be caused by the same occupational risk factors. CNA Insurance puts on an excellent ergonomic training program, where it identifies four of the major occupation risk factors. The first is repetitive motion, or the number of manipulations in a given period of time (usually measured by the hour). The second is force levels, the amount of force (effort) required to perform the tasks. The third is stressful postures such as bent wrists, shoulder abduction, and rearward reaching. The fourth is direct mechanical stress. These include stresses such as forceful gripping, low frequency vibration, and using the hand as a hammer (CNA, 1991, Table 2).

The joint venture called on the services of Dr. Jay Hammet, an occupational physician who has made CTDs his specialty. During our ongoing dialog, he identified two other occupational risk factors. The first is fatigue. As muscles tire, they are more prone to injury. The higher the overtime, the higher the CTD incident rate. The second factor is stress. As stress increases, the muscles tense. Tense muscles are more prone to injury than relaxed muscles.

There are other non-occupational risk factors that contribute to CTDs. According to CNA, predisposing medical conditions, gender, age, and cigarette smoking all can be contributing factors (CNA, 1991, Table 4). Because the joint venture cannot control these factors, they will not be dealt with in this paper. The factors the joint venture can control, their attempts at controlling these factors, and the resulting cumulative trauma incident rates are discussed in detail in the next section.

CHRONOLOGY OF THE CUMULATIVE TRAUMA PROBLEM

1990 Planning

Cumulative trauma became an issue before the joint venture facility existed. The original management team rented office space in West Knoxville to use while it created the new organization. Decisions were made on everything from plant layout, proposed customer base, product mix, and production technology to management system, financial structure, and sourcing. Almost as an afterthought, cumulative trauma was brought up as a potential problem that needed to be investigated. Although the intentions were good, the pertinent expertise was not.

The first managers and engineers hired came to the joint venture with considerable abilities and skills. The success of the joint venture is a tribute to these skills. Unfortunately, none of them had any real cumulative trauma expertise, or any exposure to it. This type of experience is not a criterion normally used in selection processes.

The first five engineers hired went to Japan for five weeks of training on their production system. While there, they received actual hands-on experience on assembly and machining lines. They observed the same type of processes the joint venture would eventually install in their new facility. After the engineers returned to the joint venture, they were debriefed. Since this was the joint venture's first real exposure to the Japanese and the systems the joint venture would adapt, the debriefing was thorough and facilitated by the Human Resource Manager.

The joint venture management team had and continues to have a genuine concern for its production workers (called technicians). The engineers were asked safety and health-related questions. They expressed concerns about the working heights on the lines, but that was all. The engineers did not see evidence of other safety problems, including cumulative trauma. They thought the work was not difficult and should not pose problems for the joint venture technicians.

A few weeks after the return of the engineers, the joint venture sent thirteen technicians, their manager, and the Human Resources Manager for training. This training was similar to that of the engineers with one exception. The technicians would receive actual hands-on experience on the new assembly line that would soon be shipped to the joint venture. The Japanese furnished the joint venture their first line of equipment. After construction, they assembled and debugged the machinery prior to shipping to the joint venture.

The managers spent many days observing the processes, looking for problems. The Japanese associates they observed worked smoothly, with no apparent distress. Questions about injuries did not reveal problems. Either the Japanese were stoic about injuries or there were none. The managers tried the work themselves. Although they were considerably slower due to lack of experience, they could not see any potential problems. At that time, neither manager had real cumulative trauma expertise.

Each manager spent much of his time with the technicians on the joint venture assembly line. Working only four weeks at extremely slow line speeds, cumulative trauma was not an issue. The technicians also had the opportunity to work on the assembly and machining lines for several days. Besides being tired, the technicians did not complain about anything else. The duration of work was too short to develop cumulative trauma problems.

With the knowledge gained by both successful trips, the joint venture went about the business of building a plant. The production processes were meticulously designed to the average American height. Machinery was ordered from the Japanese. It was eventually installed in the new, totally air conditioned facility.

Each installation had a ramp-up period. During ramp-up, production is slowly increased as the lines are debugged and technicians trained. The first ramp-up lasted one year, bringing production rates from less than 10 per shift to over 300 per shift. The next ramp up lasted less than 6 months. Each succeeding installation went easier and ramp-ups are consistently shorter.

The slow first ramp-up delayed any cumulative trauma problems. The initial technicians were thoroughly trained by the Japanese in proper work techniques. The slow ramp-up allowed muscles to gradually grow accustomed to the work (called "work hardening"). There were no time pressures to meet production schedules, as shipments were not due to begin for months. All of these factors disappeared with the second line installation. As the pace increased, new employees were hired, and shipments began, the first cases of cumulative trauma appeared. As the plant grew, so did the number of new cumulative trauma cases.

During their weekly meeting in August of 1990, the joint venture management team (composed of directors, president and vice president) were informed of the growing problem. This began the joint venture's formal efforts to manage an ever-growing problem. It soon became apparent the joint venture did not have the right skills in their professional ranks to address the issues.

After the August meeting, CNA Insurance was contacted and asked to help. CNA performed a complete ergonomics survey on the joint venture facility on September 5, 1990. The resulting ergonomics report only contained fifteen recommendations. At the time of the survey, the joint venture only had one production line and a powder coating operation installed. The recommendations included tool changes, equipment modifications, material handling improvements, implementation of work rotations, work station redesign, ergonomics training for management and supervisory personnel, and a plant-wide ergonomics program (CNA, 1990). The report arrived at the joint venture in late 1990, too late for 1990 actions, but perfectly timed for initial efforts at the beginning of 1991.

1991 Efforts

The report was well received and immediate actions in 1991 seemed likely. An ergonomics committee was formed to address the issues. Besides the Human Resource Manager, the committee was composed of the plant nurse, several engineers, and the vice president of operations. Expectations were high that the problem would be quickly eliminated. Specific assignments were made and due dates established. Unfortunately expectations were not met by reality.

The Japanese did not understand the problem because they had not encountered it before and they were not very cooperative. Time after time permission to make design changes on their machines was either ignored or delayed. To compound the problem, even though forewarned, the second line came in with the same problems as the first.

In addition to time delays, lack of ergonomic training impeded the joint venture engineers' ability to understand and design the correct tooling and to make the correct machine modifications. The engineers meant well, but many times their changes created new problems and were eventually discarded. This lack of training was corrected by CNA. The joint venture sent six people to a two-day ergonomic seminar facilitated by CNA Insurance. The seminar was excellent, and the joint venture invited CNA to present the seminar at the plant site at a later date. CNA accepted and trained an additional fifteen managers, engineers, and technicians at the joint venture.

Job rotation, one of the best ways to reduce cumulative trauma, met stiff resistance from the managers and the technicians. With the second assembly line came the need for new employees. Production rates were skyrocketing. At the same time, the just-in-time production left little room for mistakes. Managers were afraid to move experienced technicians into new loops; too many mistakes could be fatal to the infant organization. In addition, technicians felt comfortable in their experienced positions. They did not have "buy in" to the rotation theory.

As 1991 progressed, the joint venture initial actions seemed effective. Figure 4 shows the CTD rates for 1991. May dropped off to zero, leading the joint venture into a false sense of security. When second line started its ramp-up, the CTD rate jumped the next month. This led to a flurry of activity.

Figure 4. 1991 Cumulative Trauma Incident Rate.

The joint venture invited CNA insurance back for another evaluation. This audit was completed in October of 1991. CNA's report contained 34 new specific recommendations. Its conclusions were used to guide the new initiatives directed by the joint venture's ergonomic committee.

On the basis of CNA's recommendations, the joint venture initiated more aggressive actions. Restructuring of the ergonomics committee resulted in a detailed, itemized, extensive list of ergonomic engineering projects. The list contained projects, the engineer assigned as prime for each project, and anticipated completion dates. The joint venture used the list for follow-up at its bi-monthly ergonomic committee meetings. Despite the engineers' best efforts, some problems proved difficult, time consuming, and expensive. A few of the major projects would eventually take two years to successfully complete.

Late in 1991, two other analyses were completed. One analysis done by the Safety and Health Coordinator, mapped all 1990 and 1991 CTDs on a plant layout. This map highlighted several new areas of concern in the second machining lines, but none in the first comparable line. To help determine why, the joint venture nurse completed a thorough ergonomic analysis of each machine for both machining and assembly lines. The form used assigned points for frequency of motion, force, posture, mechanical stressors and task duration. The higher the points, the higher the risk of cumulative trauma. According to the nurse's comparison, both lines were virtually identical. The only differences were the speed of the line and the weight of the rack bar. The second is faster (45 second *takt* time versus 60 second *takt* time) and has a heavier autopart. The joint venture felt these were the reasons for four serious CTD's on the second line in 1991 compared to zero for the first.

A new ergonomic committee was formed to deal with the problems. At the same time, the joint venture management agreed to expand the ergonomic efforts. In October, 1991 a report was distributed that detailed the joint venture's planned efforts. Key points of the plan included:

(A) Rotation: The facility would be ergonomically mapped by the Safety, Health, Environmental Coordinator and the industrial nurse. When complete, the map would be used to develop ergonomically sound rotations for each line.

(B) Work technique and training: This problem would be addressed in several ways. The employees recently trained in ergonomics were charged with identifying current ergonomic problems, and acting as resources for training and work method redesign. The pre-employment and hiring process was targeted for modification by the Human Resource Manager and the Safety, Health, Environmental Coordinator. More effort would be placed in finding the right fit between employee and the position. The Coordinator would oversee efforts at standardizing work techniques.

(C) Equipment, tools, and layout: The initial ergonomic committee composed of four engineers, one unit manager, the industrial nurse, a management associate assigned as a team leader, and the Safety, Health, Environmental Coordinator were all ergonomically trained.

They were given the task of identifying and correcting ergonomic problems with equipment, tools or machine layout.

(D) Stretching exercises: The industrial nurse worked with the joint venture's occupational physician, Dr. Hammett, to develop an exercise program for the production technician. This program would be five to seven minutes in length and targeted to the muscle groups used on the lines.

(E) Overtime: The Vice President of Operations took the responsibility for reducing the tremendous overtime requirements. This could be done by adding a third shift, by improving machine downtime, or by a combination of both.

1991 closed on a positive, optimistic note. Thorough action plans were being diligently worked on, and cumulative trauma incidents dropped dramatically in December. This feeling of euphoria was short-lived. Cumulative trauma skyrocketed during the first month of 1992.

1992 Efforts

Beginning in January 1992, major efforts continued on the projects assigned in October 1991. Despite heroic efforts, many of the projects would take time to complete and implement. Also beginning in 1992, actual-hours-worked statistics became readily available. This made it possible to track injury trends in a variety of ways including OSHA's standard method that measures incidents per 100 employees per year.

January results showed a dramatic increase in cumulative trauma rates. Undaunted, work continued on the plan formulated in October 1991. Although the basic plan was followed, refinements were made to improve results. For example, instead of a generic exercise program for the entire plant, each line would have exercises designed for their unique working environment.

The joint venture contracted with an occupational therapist to develop the exercise programs. After each set of individual exercises was developed, the targeted teams were given ergonomics training along with instructions on how and when to perform their stretching exercises. This process proved very effective, but it took time to complete.

The Human Resource Manager, developed a new policy to help reduce the potential for CTD's in new hires. His "Injury Prevention, Employee Conditioning Policy" was readily accepted and implemented by the joint venture management.

This policy limited new hires to a maximum of eight hours per day and forty hours of work per week of work for the first four weeks. The joint venture felt this time delay would help new hires become physically conditioned to their work prior to the physical demands of overtime.

Figure 5. 1992 Cumulative Trauma Incident Rate.

Pre-employment physicals already contained a thorough screening for cumulative trauma, but there was not a post-hire follow-up. The new policy corrected this problem. After four weeks of employment, new employees are scheduled for follow-up examinations by the industrial nurse. If she does not find anything wrong, the new employees are released from overtime restrictions. If concerns are found, the nurse will follow her established protocols for treatment.

Incident rates continued high through the first quarter of 1992. A paragraph from the Safety, Health, Environmental Coordinator's monthly report highlights the joint venture's ergonomic progress:

> On the positive side, there has been a considerable amount of progress made in our ergonomic efforts. Our exercise/stretching program has been started in assembly with reasonable acceptance by the technicians. The machining lines are next, targeted for April 13th and 15th. Our "Injury Prevention, Employee Conditioning Policy" was approved and implemented. There have been several major engineering efforts including "rolling conveyors," modification of the "Inspection/Packing" work station at hose [power steering hose assembly area], and design approval for a work station for receiving (Thomas, 1992).

Even though the joint venture management realized ergonomic efforts would take time to make a difference, the June jump in CTDs created a shock wave. If the June rate continued, one out of two employees would be injured during the course of one year. Although most of these injuries were not serious, this was still a dismal record by anyone's standards.

The Safety, Health, Environmental Coordinator completed another analysis of all the 1992 OSHA recordable incidents year-to-date. On the basis of the results, ergonomic efforts were slightly modified. Most problem areas were already well documented and had both short term and long term solutions in place. Analysis indicated hose assembly as a new problem area. The joint venture quickly created a new committee to deal with the ergonomic problems associated with hose assembly. The other efforts continued on schedule.

Subtle changes in philosophy were beginning to show during this period of time. Thanks largely to the efforts of the joint venture's Director of Human Resources, both upper managements in the parent companies were well aware of the joint venture's ergonomic problems. Their positive response showed itself in several ways. Instead of an indifferent attitude, the Japanese working at the joint venture became actively involved in the search for solutions. Despite a corporate cost-cutting philosophy, the American parent company approved the capital requested for ergonomic improvements in 1993. The joint venture Director of Special Projects (responsible for new lines) became proactive instead of reactive. Ergonomic improvements were designed into the assembly lines scheduled for installation late 1992. The new line scheduled for 1993 incorporated all the previously learned ergonomic lessons. The Director of Special Projects developed a 1.2 million-dollar plan for retrofitting all the old lines with major ergonomic improvements. This plan passed the American parent company's budget review process.

Ergonomic efforts continued on track during the last half of 1992. The exercise program was fully implemented. Two technicians were assigned full-time to the task of developing standardized work for the entire plant. Two-hour rotations were developed and implemented plant wide. Improved machine performance and installation of a third shift reduced overtime requirements to acceptable levels. Engineering changes continued to be implemented. Solutions were found to several major problems that seemed impossible to correct in the past.

All these efforts seemed to be working. The CTD rate trended consistently down from a high of thirteen new CTDs in June, to a low of one CTD in December. Past experience taught the joint venture not to rest on their laurels. In late November 1993, a movement began that would challenge the joint venture's current philosophy.

CULTURAL CHANGE

In a meeting with the Safety, Health, Environmental Coordinator, the Manager of Manufacturing Services expressed his growing belief that production technicians may be their own worse enemy. He described the Japanese production lines from a different perspective. The Japanese work appears fluid, smooth, non-stressed. At different stages of the assembly line, the partially assembled gears are tested for leaks. When a leak is found, the whole line is shut down. The cause of the leak is determined and corrected before the line is started up. When observing a similar line at the joint venture, the observations are quite different.

Production technicians at the joint venture appear hurried, stressed, using two to three times the force required to perform their tasks. When a partial assembly leaks at the joint venture, the norm is to try over-tightening the connections in an effort to stop the leak. If successful, the line continues with the cause of the leak undetermined. This invariably forces the technician to use excessive force on all the following assemblies to keep them from leaking. Because excessive force is a major trauma, the joint venture inadvertently overlooked a significant source of their trouble.

The U.S. corporation's Manager of Safety and Health accepted an invitation to visit the joint venture in December 1992. In his view, the joint venture was doing everything possible to reduce the cumulative trauma rate from an engineering perspective and almost everything from a systems perspective. He agreed with the Manager of Manufacturing Services thoughts on excessive force. Before the Corporate Manager of Safety and Health left the joint venture, he introduced them to a relatively new program called *The Behavior-Based Safety Process* (Krause, 1990). According to the manager, this program would address the joint venture's new concerns as well as strengthen the overall safety program.

The Manager of Manufacturing Services and the Safety, Health, Environmental Coordinator proposed implementing this new program at the joint venture. The Plant Safety Committee along with the joint venture management readily agreed. The new program would be an addition to the other continuing ergonomic efforts in 1993.

Extensive efforts to reduce cumulative trauma rates at the joint venture met with mixed results. The Japanese production philosophies, the joint venture management system, and the American macho work ethic all played a part in creating the problems and in delaying their solutions. To understand why, each ergonomic effort will be discussed separately.

Engineering Changes

The Toyota Production System described at the beginning was a major contributor to the ergonomic problems at the joint venture. The individual machines and movement from machine to machine required technicians to perform many repetitive tasks. The short *takt* times required these tasks to be performed at high rates of speed. Some of the machines required excessive force in addition to repetitive motions. To further complicate the situation, the initial assembly lines were purchased from Japan and came fully equipped. The furnished hand tools were built to Japanese standards and were too small for American hands. Material handling techniques were implemented without ergonomic consideration.

When cumulative trauma injuries first appeared in 1990, the joint venture was in the middle of major ramp-up and expansion. Engineering was stretched to the limit trying to debug existing lines, installing new lines, and designing future lines. The joint venture management faced a continuous battle with the Japanese parent company on proper manning levels. Because production lagged behind installation, the Japanese felt the joint venture was top heavy, and would not readily agree to staff increases. The resulting compromises left the joint venture professional staff continually undermanned and overworked. Initial priorities were to get production up and running.

Even in this environment engineering changes progressed, but at a slow pace. The Japanese did not understand the joint venture's cumulative trauma problem and resisted changes to their equipment. When new assembly lines were ordered from Japan with ergonomic changes, the new lines came in identical to the old line, with no changes.

When small modifications were made to the lines, they occasionally met resistance from the technicians. The joint venture management system is team-based and encourages decisions and accountability at the technician level. Technicians felt production and quality were top priorities. They did not understand cumulative trauma and resisted anything new that may slow down production. Several times an engineer would install a device to automate a manual task. The team on shift would be given instructions and explanations on the new device. Unfortunately, this communication was not passed onto the next shift.

Faced with a new tool they did not understand, invariably the next shift would remove it (disable it) and return to the old method. Not only did this hurt the technicians, but it also had a de-motivating effect on the engineer.

Over time, the constant communication efforts of the Director of Human Resources, the Safety, Health, Environmental Coordinator and others had a positive effect on the Japanese. They became willing partners in the joint venture's attempts at curbing their growing cumulative trauma problem. Training, improved communications, and inclusion of technicians in the various cumulative trauma efforts improved technician acceptance to change.

The growing number of cumulative trauma cases began to affect production. This raised the line managers' awareness and played a major role in modifying their priorities. The new priorities of the managers allowed the engineers to place a higher priority on ergonomics. At the same time the joint venture received a new Vice President of Operations. He was a breath of fresh air to the ergonomic initiatives. The new Vice President placed the safety and health of the joint venture as his top priority.

Overall, the engineering changes have been a success story, but because of the reasons listed above, too slow in implementation. Major changes to material handling systems have eliminated cumulative trauma incidents in this area. The newest assembly lines are relatively risk free. Retrofits to the existing assembly lines and the completion of other planned changes in 1993 will eliminate all their major ergonomic contributors. The two initial lines have also seen extensive modifications. The new line will have many more improvements that will be retrofitted into the existing lines. Hose assembly is a new problem area and has an extremely active committee working on the cumulative trauma issues.

The most pressing engineering problem facing the joint venture today is maintaining ergonomic focus over an extended period of time. This same problem shows itself in other the joint venture ergonomic efforts.

Production Related Changes

The single most effective change to reduce cumulative trauma at the joint venture seems to be job rotation. When designed properly, and followed consistently, job rotations ". . . reduce the duration of exposure of any one technician to tasks that call for stressful postures, forces, and/or highly repetitive activities involving the arm, wrist, and/or hand" (Thomas, 1991). Implementation of job rotations on a two-hour schedule was not easy.

Analyzing each line and determining the proper rotation was a time consuming task. This was later expanded to include rotating the entire line through all of the different jobs. Defining the rotations was just part of the problem, gaining acceptance and implementation proved to be an uphill struggle. The Japanese felt rotations would jeopardize quality, and did not support the original efforts. Technicians placed production as their highest priority. They felt comfortable in their original jobs and resisted movement to new, unfamiliar jobs. They felt movement would hurt production and quality. With the high production volumes, technicians claimed there was not time for training. This attitude would prevail until 1992 when the line managers changed their own priorities.

Increasing cases of cumulative trauma were having negative consequences on the production lines. Many injured employees were working under stiff medical restrictions that curbed overtime and restricted the tasks the injured employee could perform. This put increasing pressures on the remaining technicians. The increasing pressure combined with intensive cumulative trauma training and improved communications succeeded in changing the manager's priorities. With the change in priority came implementation of job rotations.

Unfortunately, the joint venture team system continues to create problems with the rotation system. Team leaders are encouraged to make decisions regarding their team's production and quality. When production falls behind, or there are quality problems, some team leaders stop rotations and place their best technicians in their best jobs. This does speed up production slightly, but invariably someone pays the price with a new cumulative trauma injury. When brought to the manager's attention, the situation is corrected temporarily, until the next production or quality crisis. Until the team system is modified to hold team leaders and technicians accountable for these types of unsafe decisions, this problem will not disappear.

Another production related change is standardized work. Two dedicated production employees (trainers) have spent more than a year systematically developing standardized work sheets for each job. The process they used gained initial acceptance from the technicians.

The two trainers would follow these steps for each job:

(1) Observe the task.
(2) Perform the task.
(3) Write an initial description of the tasks.
(4) Check with technicians performing the job to assure accuracy.
(5) Include technicians and team leaders in discussions involving potential changes to routine.

(6) Involve the Safety, Health, Environmental Coordinator from an ergonomic standpoint.
(7) Involve the line engineer from a production standpoint.
(8) Write a draft based on steps one through seven.
(9) Repeat steps four through eight as many times as necessary to address everyone's concerns.
(10) Write a final draft and send it through an extensive approval process.
(11) Train team leaders and technicians in the approved standardized work.
(12) Follow-up at a later date to assure continued compliance.

The standardized work program is excellent. Its one potentially fatal flaw is similar to the other problems listed in this chapter. The existing team system does not have a method for holding team leaders and technicians accountable for following standardized work. Follow-up audits confirm this, showing only 66% compliance with standardized work. Americans are highly individualistic and with no restraints will do things their way rather than the prescribed way. Unfortunately, this individualistic behavior is a current contributor to cumulative trauma injuries. It also affects the third part of the joint venture's ergonomic initiatives--medically related changes.

Medically Related Changes

Due to the large numbers of CTD's experienced at the joint venture, the medical protocols are well defined. The joint venture is blessed with an excellent occupational nurse, a superb occupational physician who specializes in cumulative trauma, and a dedicated, caring human resources department. Because of their combined expertise, initial intervention, treatment, follow-up treatment, and the work restriction policy, they are considered among the best in the industry. Although the joint venture has experienced an alarming number of CTD's, their medical program has limited the severity and cost of most of these injuries (Dr. J. Hammett, personal communications, January 1993).

Despite their best efforts, one program initiated by the medical department has only met with limited success. The exercise program faced opposition from the beginning. The occupational therapist hired to implement this program ran into stiff resistance from some of the technician teams. A few technicians felt it was "silly" to stretch their fingers, hands and shoulders before work and at various times during work. Training explaining why these exercises were so important helped, but there were still pockets of resistance.

Exercising prior to work in Japan is an expected way of life. Because the exercises are more generic than the program custom designed for the joint venture, they may be less beneficial. According to the joint venture employees who visited the manufacturing facility in Japan, the exercises were consistently done, although with varying degrees of energy. This is not the case at the joint venture.

After all the joint venture teams had their initial training, most of them followed the exercise program. The decrease in cumulative trauma rates in 1992 can be partially attributed to these exercises. As with other programs, the success of this program rests with the team leaders and technicians. As with other programs, the lack of follow-up and accountability has spelled a slow doom for this program. As time progresses, more teams quit doing the exercises. Team leaders do not perceive that their managers consider this program important. Unless perceptions are changed, accountability and follow-up implemented, this very beneficial program will eventually disappear. These issues, common in all of the programs, will be addressed in the joint venture's 1993 effort.

1993 Effort

The joint venture will continue all their current major ergonomic efforts with one addition. They will design and implement the joint venture version of *The Behavior-Based Safety Process* (Krause, 1990). This process is designed for a total safety program, but key elements of it address the current problems associated with the joint venture's ergonomic efforts. The process itself is similar to the joint venture's quality improvement process (Krause, p.7).

The joint venture is similar to most current industries, they are reactive, not proactive. They respond to a problem to correct the problem. A behavior-based safety program combines safety into the total quality management program. It focuses on behaviors, not attitudes or incidents. Behaviors are measurable and successful behavioral change improves attitude (Krause, p.15).

This behavior-based approach is based on the premise that unsafe behaviors lead to minor accidents. Minor accidents lead to major accidents, and major accidents eventually lead to lost-time accidents. Statistically, the more lost-time accidents, the greater the chances of having an industrial related death. The more unsafe behaviors an organization has, the number of accidents at each succeeding level of severity also increases (Krause, 1990).

The behavior-based program is intensive and takes a high commitment from the joint venture management for proper implementation and follow-up. It builds on the joint venture's strengths, and helps eliminate their weaknesses. If implemented properly, it will strengthen their overall safety program as well as eliminate the problems associated with their current ergonomic initiatives (follow-up and accountability).

The joint venture is waging a long, costly battle against a stubborn and resistant problem. Japanese philosophy is embodied in the Production System. American philosophy is embodied in the joint venture team-based management system. The combination of these two systems made the joint venture an extremely successful supplier of the highest quality steering gears produced in the USA. Unfortunately these systems and Japanese and American cultural differences created an atmosphere that not only fostered cumulative trauma injuries, but proved remarkably resistant to intensive corrective measures.

The most recent statistics show continuing cumulative trauma incidence (CTI), but at lower rates. Incidents of cumulative trauma fell during 1992 as employees sought ways to reduce them, but jumped again in January 1993 despite new procedures. Only in the second half of 1993 do cumulative trauma incidents begin to drop towards a tolerable level.

The rise in cumulative trauma injuries directly corresponds to the problems discussed earlier in this chapter. As production team leaders reduce their enforcement of exercise programs, rotations, and standardized work, the cumulative trauma injury rate increases.

The Production System problems have been identified. Most of them have been corrected. The remaining problems have action plans and targeted completion dates. More importantly, the joint venture Japanese partners finally realize the severity of the problem and are active partners in the search for solutions. The two cultures will never be identical, but once understood, differences can be overcome.

The lack of follow-up and the lack of team leader accountability continue to plague some of the current ergonomic initiatives. Excellent programs such as job rotation, standardized work, and team exercises will continue to diminish in importance until accountability and follow-up is improved. The new behavior-based safety approach should eliminate these problems. Two keys to the program, measuring and charting, are two strengths of the Joint Venture Production System. Two other keys to the new program, follow-up and accountability, are current weaknesses at the joint venture.

The lessons learned in this joint venture were at times painful, sometimes difficult to solve, and always time consuming. The blend of cultures has been a learning experience for both the Americans and the Japanese. The end result is a highly successful company. With the programs implemented in 1993, the joint venture is not only highly successful but also fosters a safe and healthy environment for all the employees.

REFERENCES

CNA Insurance (1991). [Occupational ergonomics for engineers]. Unpublished raw data.

Ellis, W. (1986). *Japan and I.* Murfreesboro, TN: The Japan Center.

Fucini, J. J., & Fucini, S. F. (1990). *Working for the Japanese: Inside Mazda's American auto plant.* New York: The Free Press.

Konz, S. (1990). *Work design: Industrial ergonomics* (3rd ed.). Worthington: Publishing Horizons.

Krause, T. R., Hidley, J. H., & Hodson, S.J. (1990). *The behavior-based safety process: Managing involvement for an injury-free culture.* New York: Van Nostrand Reinhold.

Love, R. (1992). [Principles of ergonomics]. Unpublished raw data. Occupational Safety and Health Administration (1990). *Ergonomics program management recommendations for general industry.* Washington, DC: Superintendent of Documents.

Putz-Anderson, V. (1988). *Cumulative trauma disorders: A manual for musculoskeletal diseases of the upper limbs.* London: Taylor & Francis.

Thomas, L. W. (1988). *Preliminary selection and training plan.* Unpublished booklet.

Thomas, L. W. (1991). [Ergonomic activity report]. Unpublished report.

Thomas, L. W. (1992). [March monthly report for safety health environmental] Unpublished report.

Chapter 3

ATTITUDES TOWARD JAPANESE INVESTMENT IN EAST TENNESSEE*

*Scott Brunger*** *and Young-Bae Kim*

U.S. ATTITUDES TOWARD JAPANESE INVESTMENT

Japanese investment in the United States provokes ambivalent feelings. On the one hand, articles in business publications proclaim "The buying of America: Is danger lurking?" (McClenahen, 1990, p.62) in *Industry Week* or trumpet "How the Japanese got burned in the USA (losing money and goodwill)" (Thornton, 1992, p.114) in *Fortune*. On the other hand, when new Japanese investment flows dry up, the business community worries that the United States has a deteriorating investment climate too, as in "Japanese wary of U.S. operations" (Holman, 1992, p.A15) in *The Wall Street Journal* or "Japan to scale back" (1992, pp.1,20) in *Automotive News*.

Part of the ambivalence may result because foreign investment has different consequences for different interest groups in society. Industry competitors and the communities dependent on their jobs fear for their interests, so they criticize

---

* Portions of this paper were presented at the Southern Regional Japan Studies Seminar in Atlanta, Georgia, April 27, 1991 and published in *Current Politics and Economics of Japan*, Vol. 2:1, pp.1-4, 1992.

** The authors wish to thank Denise Franklin, Maria Hawkins and Rose McNabb for telephone interviewing and James Gomez and Rachel Moore for secretarial assistance as well as Dr. John Nichols for statistical advice.

successful foreign enterprises using the rhetoric of nationalism. Potential clients and communities hosting new foreign companies appreciate the opportunities offered by the foreign investment and express publicly their support. Neither side is confused about its own interests, though the public debate may be ambivalent.

The public debate on foreign investment resulted in pressure in 1988 by the U.S. Congress for disclosure of foreign ownership, the Exon-Florio Amendment. According to U.S. Government publications, Japanese direct investment measured at historical cost rose to U.S. $97 billion in 1992 passing for the first time the United Kingdom as the largest foreign source of capital. However, only half the Japanese investment was in industry and of that $19 billion in manufacturing. The United Kingdom still led with $42 billion in manufacturing, while the Netherlands came second with $21 billion in 1992 ("Foreign Direct Investment," July 1993, p.64). Clearly Japanese investment is not crucial to U.S. prosperity, though it is important in some industries, notably motor vehicles, and in the industrial heartland of the Midwest, where much of the public outcry originated.

Future prospects for growth of Japanese motor vehicle production in the United States are great enough that they will continue to attract public attention. In an article in the *Journal of Policy Modeling*, Gerard Adams et al. predict that by 1996 Japanese transplant auto manufacturing would produce 3.3 million vehicles out of a total of 16.3 million in the United States. Japanese transplants will provide directly 22,000 U.S. jobs within their factories. Through U.S. purchases that reach 85% domestic content in the vehicles, projections reach a total of 76,000 manufacturing jobs or 0.2% of GNP. (Winter 1991, pp.469, 483).

Continued growth of Japanese motor vehicle production representing an important sector of the U.S. economy will remain an issue of public debate. That debate feeds back into community attitudes that affect the productivity of Japanese investments.

Local community attitudes as in this study remain an important factor in future growth of foreign investment.

Review of Literature on Attitudes to Foreign Investment

Foreign manufacturing investment in Appalachia represents a double challenge since it is both foreign and urban. While most studies of citizen attitudes to new development have been made in the Western United States, one exception is a study of "Attitudes towards New Development in Three Appalachian

Counties" by Trent, Stout-Weigand and Smith. They show that three West Virginia valley communities favor economic development in the form of tourism, manufacturing, shopping centers, farming and forestry. Reticence is towards polluting industries, such as strip-mining, coke plants, and clear-cutting forests. Their responses correspond with those below in our study. We add the option to "Keep Blount Country the way it is," though most prefer to see expansion in farming, tourism, manufacturing, services, and government installations.

Past studies of attitude to foreign investment show it is positively correlated with educational level, income and occupational status. Pitman and Choe studied shopping mall respondents to discover their attitudes to Japanese investments and products. They found that education, income and status are positively related to tolerance for foreign investment as are acceptance of Japanese companies in America to make us more productive, and acknowledgment of superior Japanese products. They also discovered that the three variables reduce beliefs that Japanese investors cause inflation or unemployment or represent a threat. They explain their findings on the grounds that upper class people have more knowledge and control of their situation so they can appreciate the opportunity to meet foreigners, while lower class people are more likely to be suspicious of foreigners and foreign products (p.16). Our study finds similar correlations below.

Hougland in a study of the county surrounding the Kentucky Toyota plant found significant relationships between education ($probability<.001$) and income ($p<.01$) and expectations of benefits to the community from the Japanese auto factory. He found a significant negative relation to years in county ($p<.001$) and by female respondents ($p<.05$). A favorable expectation about the company's hiring practices and a positive attitude toward the county also related to favorable opinions about Toyota ($p<.001$).

The presence of a new factory may cause favorable attitudes in the local population because local businesses believe that they would be able to sell their products and services to it. However, the prospect that a new factory in a region might attract new suppliers and customers does not seem hopeful. According to o hUallachain, previous studies of foreign industry in the Republic of Ireland and Washington State indicate that the major economic impact occurs from the payment of wages and salaries, though foreign ownership does not necessarily lead to fewer inter-industry linkages than domestic ownership (p.156).

Denso (formerly Nippondenso) is already integrated with the production system of the Toyota factory in Kentucky. Existing Tennessee companies are unlikely to subcontract for Denso, since to do so requires a high degree of dependency on production hierarchy, which only specialized firms would be likely to accept.

Nor does the prospect of Denso attracting new business services seem promising. Cocheba, Gilmer and Mack point out that branch plants in non-metropolitan areas in the South do not attract business services. Their study finds producer service employment and earnings negatively related to manufacturing production, while positively related to corporate headquarters employment and earnings (p.60). Since Knoxville is not a major corporate headquarters center in the South, the presence of another blue-collar plant fifteen miles away diminishes prospects for it becoming one.

Instead, the emphasis must be placed on the effect of new consumer demand in the region (o hUallachain). The increase of 2% in total consumer demand resulting from the new factories represents their principal economic impact in the community. In 1997, the 90 Japanese managers represent an easily identifiable new source of demand that is 2% of the income group earning over $50,000 per year.

Payment of property taxes by the foreign company is another way that the community benefits. Denso is the largest single taxpayer representing 22.6% of city property taxes in 1991-92 (City of Maryville Audit). Though property taxes only represent one-third of municipal revenues, the payment of sales and property taxes by Denso employees is also important.

SURVEY AND INTERVIEW METHODS

Findings are based on a telephone survey from January 21 to February 7, 1991. No news stories on Denso or Japanese investments appeared during that period that might alter public opinions. The survey used a random sample from phone book of 225 names with 144 respondents. Although the phone book does not include all possible households, it includes those likely to be politically active.

Press coverage of the Denso factory has been extensive. The daily paper claims to reach 80% of the homes in the county. Its effectiveness is demonstrated by the fact that any Asian is assumed to be Japanese from Denso, including the Korean-American writing this chapter. The paper has a favorable editorial position on foreign investment and economic development which may not necessarily be shared by its readership, however.

The income distribution in Maryville and Alcoa is such that Japanese expenditure patterns represent an important addition to demand in upscale stores. Shopkeepers can easily identify them and expect that word of mouth will influence other Japanese to come. Smaller foreign firms from Britain, Canada, Germany and Sweden have less impact and visibility.

In order to find out whether businesses consider the Denso plant provides them entrepreneurial opportunities, the authors interviewed several local retail businesses to learn about their responses to the presence of an upscale Japanese population. The sample is not random, since many businesses are unlikely to see effects of the presence of a Japanese company. For example, to the chagrin of autosellers, Denso arranged to lease cars. Local dealers expected to sell cars.

In business interviews the authors assume that a change in the environment, presence of an identifiable new group of consumers, would motivate entrepreneurial response. This response is influenced by perception of success elsewhere, cross-cultural experience and training.

The difficulty of carrying out a telephone survey and business interviews is one of timing. The authors hesitated to interview businesses during the construction period of the plant, because they wanted to avoid tainting the telephone survey. However, when the telephone survey was conducted, business attitudes had hardened. The interviews then do not indicate whether current attitudes reflect pre-dispositions that influenced firms to alter their practices to attract Japanese consumers or reflect the results of experience after the arrival of Japanese consumers.

FINDINGS

Among the respondents to the sample, 57% were women. The majority were married. The average age was in the forties with over twenty years spent in the county. Their average income was $23,000 and educational level twelfth grade. 85% read newspapers and watch television regularly. 40% had traveled abroad.

This study attempts to explain local attitudes towards foreign investment in general and towards Japanese investment in particular. Both sets of attitudes correlate well with theoretical expectations, though attitude towards foreign investment is more favorable than towards Japanese investment. Just over half of the respondents agreed they "believe more foreign-owned companies should be invited to come into our community" and under half would invite more Japanese-owned companies. These results compare to a Wall Street Journal/ NBC News poll, which found "69% of registered voters said the Japanese already invest 'too much' in the United States" (WSJ, June 19, 1990, p.1). The difference might be that residents of a small city feel better about Japanese investment located in their community than located elsewhere in the United States.

To see whether demographic variables relate to attitudes in favor of more foreign investment or more Japanese investment in the community, Pearson's product-moment correlations are given in Table 1. The symbol * indicates a probability level of 95% or more, while ** indicates a probability level over 99%.

Table 1. Demographic Variables and Investment

	Correlation Coefficients	
	More Foreign Inv.	More Japanese Inv.
Demographic Variables		
Education by grade completed	.24**	.33**
Income by ten thousand $	.23**	.23**
Age by decade	-.26**	-.38**
Travel	.16*	.09
Female Gender	-.12**	-.10

As expected, education and income are highly correlated to favorable attitudes to foreign and Japanese investment. Age is negatively correlated with attitude to foreign investment and to Japanese investment. Since older Americans are more likely to remember World War II and postwar reconstruction, such a finding is expected.

As in Pitman and Choe's study, people who have traveled abroad also have a more favorable attitude to foreign investment, though less so to Japanese investment. Such people have higher incomes and education, so perhaps their higher social status leads them to favor foreign investment.

As in the study of Toyota in Kentucky, our study shows men more than women favor more foreign investment. Even though men in the sample are younger and have traveled abroad more than women, they still favor outside investment when those two factors are controlled. To show the independent effect of each of these demographic factors, the results of a multiple linear regression are given in Table 2. Explanatory variable -- sex, education, age, income, and travel abroad--show that the difference between men's and women's attitudes towards foreign investment and Japanese investment appears significant.

Table 2. Regression on Foreign/Japanese Investment

Dependent Variable	Constant	Explanatory Variables				R2	F-Value
		Female	Age	Education	Income		
More Foreign Investment	1.54**	-0.63**	-0.14*	0.09	0.09	.23	8.4
More Japanese Investment	1.56**	-0.38*	-0.23**	0.12	0.08	.24	8.9

The symbol * indicates a probability level of 95% or more, while ** indicates a probability level over 99%.

Female gender lowers significantly the probability that the respondent will be favorable to foreign or Japanese investment. Also each decade of age lowers the favorable attitude toward foreign or Japanese investment. Education and income level raises it, though not significantly in this regression.

Unlike the Toyota study, where years spent in the Kentucky County correlate negatively with support for foreign investment, this Tennessee study does not show that years in county are significant. Longtime residents of the county appear to reject some of the forms of economic development favored in the West Virginia study. Years spent in the county correlate negatively with preferences for farming, tourism, manufacturing, and government installations (all $p<.05$). However, they respond negatively also to "keep it the way it is." Actually the answer "keep it the way it is" correlates highly with economic development in all the other areas ($p<.01$) so that perhaps respondents do not understand it as a rejection of economic development. Age itself was significantly correlated only with rejection of government installations ($p<.05$). Apparently longtime residents are more suspicious of forms of economic development than others.

Parents with children in school have favorable attitudes to foreign investment and Japanese investment ($p<.05$). The school system has programs to promote tolerance and Japanese families have been faithful participants in parents' organizations, so parents may have favorable experiences. The school system has organized Japanese language classes as an option for American students. However, those factors do not explain why families would favor foreign investment more than Japanese. The more likely explanation is that people in this sample with school-age children have higher incomes and traveled more than others ($p<.05$).

Personal opinions are also highly correlated to attitudes about foreign investments as in Table 3.

Table 3. Opinion Variables and Investment

Opinion Variables	More Foreign Investment	More Japanese Investment
Foreign investment threat?	-.39**	-.35**
Any foreign company can invest?	.20**	.27**
Strengthens US economy?	.23**	.19**
Foreign invest. creates jobs?	.32**	.26**
Lose control?	-.36**	-.39**
Economy needs Japanese invest.?	.39**	.37**
Name foreign investment in cty	.25**	.23**
Own Foreign Products?	.31**	.29**
Is U.S. status declining?	-.24**	-.18*
Resent "selling America"?	-.39**	-.43**
Want to work at Denso?	-.04	.02

* indicates .05 probability level, ** .01 probability level

Those who believe "foreign investment in the United States is a threat to the country" uniformly reject it in the county ($p<.01$). Those who believe "any foreign company with the financial ability should be allowed to invest in the United States" accept it ($p<.01$). Those who favor foreign and Japanese investment in the United States agree that "it strengthens the U.S. economy" ($p<.01$) and that "it creates jobs" ($p<.01$) while they disagree that "it leads the U.S. to lose control over its destiny" ($p<.01$) and are "concerned more than before about the declining status of the U.S. economy in the world" ($p<.01$).

Those who can name foreign-owned businesses in Blount County are favorable to foreign and Japanese investment ($p<.01$). Awareness of ownership of foreign products also is related highly to acceptance of foreign investment ($p<.01$). Those who believe that "Japanese products are superior to American products" accept Japanese investment ($p<.05$).

The questionnaire gives an opportunity to describe Japanese in five words. Only half the respondents answer the question. They generally describe traits much admired by Americans, e.g. Japanese dedication, discipline, cleverness, education and courtesy. Only one-tenth mention negative traits and these are the bad side of positive traits, e.g. ruthlessness (dedication), shrewdness (cleverness), and sneakiness (courtesy that obscures intentions). Apparently the public has a clear stereotype of Japanese, whom most admire, though some fear.

The local newspaper and television have been favorable to foreign investment, though customers do not share the same opinions. Most newspaper readers "believe foreign investment in the United States is too much" ($p<.05$). For one thing, the readers are older ($p<.01$) and favor farming for the future of Blount County ($p<.1$). At the same time they claim to have traveled more ($p<.01$) and have a higher income ($p<.05$), both of which normally correlate favorably with outside investment. Similarly, the television viewers disagree that "any foreign company with the financial ability should be allowed to invest in the United States" ($p<.1$). Apparently the newspaper and television shape the opinions of their customers less than other influences.

Interest in finding a job at Denso is not correlated with acceptance of Japanese investment. The Hougland study of Toyota indicated job prospects affect attitudes. In our study the desire for a job at Denso is negatively correlated with education ($p<.01$) and with income ($p<.05$), so other factors may obscure the effect of job prospects on attitudes. In Table 4, a multiple regression show the independent effects of each of these factors on attitudes to foreign investment and Japanese investment.

Table 4. Regression on Foreign/Japanese Investment

Dependent Variable	Constant	Explanatory Variables				R2	F-Value
		No Job	Education	Income	Female		
More Foreign Investment	1.21**	-0.68**	0.10	0.07	-0.63*	.27	8.2
More Japanese Investment	0.75**	-0.54*	-0.14*	0.07	-0.37*	.18	5.0

The symbol * indicates 95% probability level, while ** indicate 99% probability level.

In Table 4 lack of job prospects at Denso (No Job) is negatively related to attitudes towards more foreign and more Japanese investment ($p<.01$). Also the higher the educational level, the higher the acceptance of foreign and Japanese investment. The higher the income, the higher the acceptance. As in Table 3 female gender is negatively related to attitudes to foreign investment and Japanese investment.

Interviews with local businesses reveal that publicity about the coming of Denso created some expectations that have not been realized, often because the businesses had not familiarized themselves with Japanese customs. For example, a local realtor pointed out that brokers expected to sell houses to the Japanese, who preferred to rent instead. Since brokerage fees here for rental equal one-month's rent, brokers were not interested in finding houses and ignored the market. Japanese respondents indicate they are accustomed to paying higher agency fees for rentals.

Other local businesses successfully made adjustments in their lines. An upscale supermarket in the area attracted Japanese patronage by emphasizing customer service and variety. It introduced thin-sliced meat, special seafood, and oriental vegetables. The store is looking for a reliable supplier of Japanese packaged foods, but had some bad experiences.

Another example is a trendy women's clothing boutique in the shopping mall, which introduced smaller sizes and international brand names. They emphasize service, translate their fashion shows into Japanese, notify a mailing list of coming sales and find their Japanese customers very responsive.

Some businesses have made money the old-fashioned way. A well established bank attracted the accounts of Denso employees. A manager claims the bank initiated no special program or gave special training to staff to handle their transactions. He is right, since the tellers still find a Japanese passport to be inadequate identification. He describes Japanese as "good customers." A rival bank claims that political connections gave the other bank the Denso business. However, they also assume consumer banking would not be profitable, since Japanese do not borrow money for homes or cars.

In general after the announcement of the Denso plant created high expectations in the local business community, there followed either disillusionment when no increase in sales occurred or quiet satisfaction at successful attraction of new customers. After business opinion has gone through this cycle, it is impossible for researchers to distinguish whether the former businesses began with unrealistic attitudes towards Japanese customers, while the latter had more open attitudes and therefore succeeded.

CONCLUSION

The random survey of public opinion in a Tennessee county confirms the hypotheses that higher income and education levels are positively related to acceptance of Japanese investment, while age is negatively related. No confirmation came for the hypothesis that belief in manufacturing as a way of progress leads to higher acceptance of a foreign manufacturing firm. Nor were belief in farming, tourism, services or government significantly correlated with acceptance of a foreign manufacturing firm.

Interviews with local businesses about their attempts to attract Japanese customers reveal very mixed results. Feelings about these results overclouded information about their cultural sensitivity, perception of business opportunity, and cross-cultural experiences. The interviews do not indicate whether previous attitudes prompt a firm to take an entrepreneurial view of the presence of Japanese or a "business as usual" one.

This survey suggests several policies for civic leaders to accommodate Japanese manufacturing plants:

(1) Do not stress Japanese ownership of the plant, since foreign investment is more favorably regarded than Japanese investment. Communities often have factories owned by outside interests and learn to live with them. When initial announcements make claims for prosperity for local people that does not occur quickly, disillusionment sets in. Press scrutiny, even when favorable, seems to create social distance between the company and community rather than improving public attitudes towards the company.

(2) Identify the foreign company with the community. At least in a small city public attitudes towards foreign firms seem to depend on civic pride rather than personal benefits through a job or business contacts. Denso identified with the community by distributing company families widely among suburbs, sending children to public schools, encouraging managers to join civic clubs, and contributing to local charities. Through identification, the public views companies in their own community as better than those same companies elsewhere.

(3) Emphasize the many Japanese characteristics that Americans admire, such as dedication, discipline, cleverness, courteousness, and education.

(4) To avoid envy, local officials should pay attention to locally owned businesses as well as outside firms. As many jobs can be lost when a local company leaves or fails to expand as when outside companies arrive. Local officials should also prepare for extensive negotiations with Japanese firms before agreement is reached. These negotiations require detailed documentation and support from many agencies of government, the Chamber of Commerce, and members of the business community. The negotiations are a worthwhile investment since as the director of the Chamber states "Once you arrive at mutual understanding, there is a lot of trust" (Bill Dunavant, personal communication, July 23, 1993).

Interview Questionnaire

Interviewer ________________ Phone Number _________________

Hello. My name is ____________. I am at Maryville College making a survey of citizen attitudes towards economic development in our community. I would like to ask you some questions about your opinion (not to sell anything).

Demographics

1) Sex: Male 0 Female 1

2) Age: teens 0, 20s 2, 30s 3, 40s 4, 50s 5, 60s or above 6

3) Marital status: single 0 Married 1 Divorced 2 Widowed 3

4) How many years have you lived in Blount County?
   <10 1, 10-20 2, 20-30 3, 30-40 4, 40-50 5, 50+ 6

5) Do you read newspaper(s) regularly? Yes 2,Occasionally 1, No 0

6) Do you watch TV news regularly? Yes 2,Occasionally 1, No 0

7) Do you own products (such as automobile, TV, stereo, kitchen appliances, etc.) made by foreign companies? Yes 2, No 0

Attitudes

8) Do you believe that Japanese products are superior to American products?
   Yes 2 Same 1 No 0

9) In the future would you prefer the following parts of the Blount County economy to grow or would you like to keep Blount county the way it is?
   Keep it the way it is Yes 2, No 0
   Farming growth Yes 1 No 0 Services growth Yes 1, No 0
   Tourism growth Yes 1 No 0 Government Yes 1, No 0
   Manufacturing Yes 1 No 0 (airport, military, etc.)

10) Name the foreign country you think has the largest investment in the United States?

Britain 2, Japan 1, Other 0

11) Do you believe foreign investment in the United States is :

Too much 2, Just right 1, Too little 0, No opinion ___

12) Should any foreign company with the financial ability be allowed to invest in the United States? Yes 2 No 0 No opinion__

13) Do you believe that foreign investment in the United States is a threat to the country? Yes 2 No 0 No opinion__

14) Why do you think the United States relies on foreign capital?

____

15) Is any particular country's investment in the United States more worrisome than another country's investment? Yes__ No__

If yes, which one? Japan 1 Other 0 Why?______________________

16) What do you believe foreign investment is doing in the United States economy?

It strengthens the U.S. economy.	Yes 1	No 0
It leads the U.S. to lose control over its destiny.	Yes 1	No 0
It creates cultural and racial conflict.	Yes 1	No 0
It holds interest rate down and creates jobs.	Yes 1	No 0
It helps reduce our trade deficit.	Yes 1	No 0

17) Do you believe that the U.S. needs Japanese investment to keep the economy strong?

Yes 1 No 0

18) Are you aware of foreign-owned companies in Blount County?

Yes 1 No 0 If yes, which ones ________________________________

19) How do you believe Denso has affected or will affect our community?

They will strengthen the area economy.	Yes 1	No 0
They will create cultural conflict.	Yes 1	No 0
They are going to take us over.	Yes 1	No 0
They will enrich cultural life in the community.	Yes 1	No 0

20) Do you believe more foreign-owned companies should be invited to come into our community? Yes 1 No 0

21) Do you believe more Japanese-owned companies should be invited to come into our community? Yes 1 No 0

22) How has the presence of Denso affected you in the following areas:

become a better informed citizen Yes 1 No 0
become interested in learning more about foreign culture Yes 1 No 0
become more concerned than before about the declining status of the U.S. economy Yes 1 No 0
resent selling of America to Japanese Yes 1 No 0

23) Would you like to work at Denso if you were given an opportunity?
Yes 1 No 0 Why?___________

24) Give five words which you believe best describe Japanese

___________ _____________ __________ ___________ _____________

Demographics

25) Level of education completed: number of years of schooling ___

26) Occupation: _____________

27) Household income:
<10K 0 10-19K 1 20-29K 2 30-39K 3 40-49K 4 50+K 5

28) Number of school-age children at home _____

29) Traveled abroad: Yes 1 No 0

30) Exposure to foreign culture through: None 0, Study 1, Foreign friend 2, living overseas 3, marriage 4

REFERENCES

Adams, Gerard, Byron Gagnes & Gene Huang "*Journal of Policy Modeling* Winter 1991, pp.467-88.

Barlik, Timothy, Charles Becker, Steve Lake and John Rush "Saturn and State Economic Development" *Forum for Applied Research and Public Policy* Spring 1987, pp.34-39.

Butler, Iva "Welcome, Nippondenso!" *The Morning Daily Times* Oct.16, 1990.

________ "Jobs for More than 400: Nippondenso says low-level shipments have begun" *The Daily Times* June 13, 1990. City of Maryville, *City Audit 1991-92*.

Cocheba, Donald, Robert Gilmer and Richard Mack "Causes and Consequences of Slow Growth in the Tennessee Valley Service Sector" *Growth and Change* January 1986, pp.51-65.

Cole, Robert E. *Work, Mobility and Participation: A Comparative Study of American and Japanese Industry* Berkeley: University of California Press, 1979.

Cole, Robert E. and Donald R. Deskins, Jr. "Racial Factors in Site Locations and Employment Patterns of Japanese Auto Firms in America" *California Management Review* Fall 1988, pp.9-22.

"Foreign Direct Investment in the United States to 1992" *Survey of Current Business* July 1993, Vol.73(7), pp.59-88.

Gilmer, Robert "Cyclical and Structural Change in Southern Manufacturing: Recent Evidence from the Tennessee Valley" *Growth and Change* October 1986, pp.61-69.

Hill, Richard Child "Comparing Transnational Production Systems: The Automobile Industry in the USA and Japan" *International Journal of Urban and Regional Research* Fall 1990, pp.462-480.

Holman, Richard L. "Japanese Wary of U.S. Operations" *Wall Street Journal* June 9, 1992, p.Ai5.

Hougland, James G., Jr. "Toyota: A Longitudinal Analysis of Semi-Rural Industrialization" presentation at North Central Sociological Association, April 15, 1989, Akron, Ohio.

Huallacháin, Breandan "The Role of Foreign Direct Investment in the Development of Regional Industrial Systems" *Regional Studies* April 1986, pp.151-152.

"Japan to Scale Back" *Automotive News* June 22, 1992, pp.1,20.

Kawata, Makoto "Making it Work: Japanese Direct Investment in the United States" *Journal of Japanese Trade & Industry* No.1, 1984, pp.25-27.

Lehner, Urban and Alan Murray "Strained Alliance: 'Selling of America' to Japanese touches some very raw nerves" *Wall Street Journal*, June 19, 1990, p.1.

McClenahen, John S. "The Buying of America: Is Danger Lurking?" *Industry Week* June 4, 1990 vol. 238(11), pp.62-67.

Pitman, Glenn A. and Sang T. Choe "Attitudinal Variation Toward Japanese investment in the U.S." *SAM Advanced Management Journal* Summer 1989, pp.15-18.

Stone, Dean "Nippondenso Manufactures Parts for Both American and Japanese Autos" *The Morning Daily Times* January 9, 1991, p.1-2.

Thorton, Emily "How the Japanese got burned in the USA (losing money and goodwill)" *Fortune* June 15, 1992, vol.125(12), pp.114-17.

"Toyota to Apply Japan Methods to Parts Procurement in U.S." *The Japan Economic Journal*, March 21, 1987, p.20.

Trent, Roger, Nancy Stout-Weigand and Dennis Smith "Attitudes Towards New Development in Three Appalachian Counties" *Growth and Change* July 1985, pp.54-63.

U.S. Department of Commerce, Bureau of Census *County and City Data Book 1988.*

__________ *Population Census 1990.*

Chapter 4

CULTURE SHOCK AMONG JAPANESE WIVES OF BUSINESSMEN

*Manami Miura**

CULTURE SHOCK AND HOW TO COPE

Culture shock occurs when an individual confronts disorienting experiences in an unfamiliar setting. A business view of culture shock emphasizes the "stress overload" that occurs as the individual attempts to cope with "hundreds of jarring and disorienting incidents" (Copeland & Griggs, p.195). The individual suffers anxiety trying to decipher the setting, trying to react to unexpected messages from others, and trying to understand values that seem strange (Oberg, p.43).

Culture shock has many effects on the individual. Stress causes physical problems, such as eating and sleeping disorders, made worse by the aftereffects of travel across time zones or "jet lag." Also, confusion results when the environment sends strange messages and other people seem to have peculiar expectations. One's mind must work overtime to decipher the meaning of everything in terms that still make sense. One feels impotent in unfamiliar surroundings. Personal values are threatened as one discovers others do not share one's beliefs. Finally, there comes "a sense of loss . . . of friends, status, and profession" (Furnham & Bochner, p.48).

---

* Freeman Public Relations, Tokyo

The experience of culture shock can also occur within a country. As an example, in America there are many different backgrounds. If a person with a Japanese ancestry goes to a Spanish neighborhood, culture shock results. Or if a person raised in the South goes to the North, a city boy moves to a small town, or a rich girl suddenly becomes poor, all of them can have a degree of culture shock (Bassis et al, p.79). They would experience stronger symptoms, though, if they went overseas because more unfamiliar things would crowd into their experience and create stress.

Several stages of development of culture shock can be identified. A "dreaming stage" occurs in anticipation of the trip. A "honeymoon stage" begins on arrival when the traveler notices many attractive things and ignores small irritations. Then comes the "sour stage" as problems accumulate and physical sensations become uncomfortable. It is easy to get stuck in this stage. One can withdraw to the safety of one's own nationality group and avoid contact with the local culture. One can become euphoric and deny problems. One can become depressed and overcome by small matters. To get stuck makes one ineffective as well as unsatisfied in the culture. The way out is to pay attention to the culture and learn why and how things really work there. With patience after six to twelve months one reaches the "enjoyment stage" when one accepts those things one can enjoy and intentionally leaves the others (Gur & Gur, pp.196-99).

Several alternative words are also used to describe culture shock. For instance, Guthrie calls it "cultural fatigue," Byrnes "role shock," Smalley "language shock," and Ball-Rokeach "pervasive ambiguity" (cited in Furnham and Bochner, p.49). Whatever the name used to describe culture shock, the important issue is to how to reduce its effects on business.

Four strategies to minimize culture shock are presented in the literature. The first is choice of candidates with resilient personalities, who can resist effects of culture shock. Psychologists note that culture shock leads to "an increase in risk of mental and physical disorder" (Fisher, p.1). Candidate screening using physical exams and personality tests, such as the Minnesota Multiphasic Personality Inventory that indicates incipient disorder, can reduce effects of culture shock. Screening should include the family as well as the candidate, since the others may experience worse culture shock and thereby affect the performance of the candidate too.

Another way to choose personnel to send overseas is to rely on previous experience. Candidates who have adjusted before to culture shock are more likely to anticipate the many forms it will take and cope better. Having gone through culture shock before, they are less likely to get stuck before reaching the stage of enjoyment of the new culture. They are not prone to resist the new culture by acting as if they had "never left home," or to repudiate their own culture by "going native" (Furnham & Bochner, pp.48-49). "Never leaving home" makes them ineffective because they refuse to compromise. "Going native" makes them ineffective because they appear to have no cultural identity of their own, so both cultures fail to respect them.

For sending business executives overseas, individuals with higher occupation, education, and income status generally adjust more successfully (Fisher, p.4). They bring more personal resources to the new situation, so they can be more confident of the results. Although business executives have careers that keep them busy, their families may not have roles in the new country that support them as much. While the executive is tied to a familiar company routine, the others cope with the new culture without support of any familiar institution. High status families can afford, though, to bring books, magazines, computer games, and videos from home that preserve their familiar identity in the new setting.

Preparation for culture shock also helps to reduce its effects. Background reading and videos about the country help provide a framework for new experiences. Language training is necessary to the level where everyone in the family can find their way, shop, read signs, and engage in polite greetings in the new situation. Nothing is more debilitating than relying on compatriots to translate everything. In order to understand the foreign culture from the inside, travelers should read novels, histories, and religious or philosophical writings. Finally, they should make plans to provide necessary escapes: how to secure emergency help, when to keep in touch with family or friends back home, and where to find groups of compatriots for relaxation at restaurants, resorts or places of worship in the new country. Most of all, the business family needs time to discuss the move, rest, and pack in an orderly manner.

In sum then, a company responsible for sending personnel overseas should:

(1) screen them carefully to avoid incipient physical or mental problems,
(2) choose those with previous experience not only in business but also in adapting to foreign cultures,
(3) support their sense of identity while encouraging them to explore the foreign culture, and
(4) provide opportunities for advanced preparation before travel.

RESULTS OF QUESTIONNAIRE ON CULTURE SHOCK

To test the hypothesis that culture shock might be difficult for family members besides the working husband, I prepared a questionnaire on culture shock for Japanese wives of businessmen. A similar questionnaire had been administered to Japanese students who showed high concern for culture shock (Hartung, Huffman). The English translation of the questionnaire is found in the end of the chapter.

In August, 1991 I distributed the questionnaire to sixty Japanese wives in English language classes that they were expected to take. Only thirty-five women returned the questionnaires, so the results given below are not a complete survey of the population. Nevertheless, in the author's opinion they are representative of the situation of most Japanese wives.

Demographic Background of the Sample

The questionnaire starts with demographics. Knowing the respondents' age is very important because I think that generally the older you get the more difficulty you have in adjusting to a new environment. Younger people are more flexible.

The reason I asked their husbands' age was to know briefly how high his position would be in the company. In a Japanese firm it is easy to estimate status simply by knowing his age because of the seniority-promotion system (Sethi, Namiki & Swanson, p.235). Husband's positions in the companies are very important to their wives because these positions would automatically become the wives' positions. Wives who have power sometimes put pressure on the other wives through advice and reprimands. If lower status wives violate standards set by bosses' wives, the women's association, called the *fujinkai*, activates an invisible judicial system to get them in trouble and their husbands too. These are all unwritten rules, but they do exist.

In the sample twelve respondents are age 36-40, nine are age 31-35, six are 26-30, and five are 41-45. Their husbands are slightly older but still mostly in mid-career. Nine are 41-45, also nine are 36-40, eight are 31-35, five are 46-50, and only two are 26-30. My hypothesis did not turn out as I expected. Both younger wives and older wives are having difficulties adjusting to American culture's foods, language, etc. I think that because younger women have small children, they do not have time to themselves to reduce stress. Also, younger women have less power, so in fact their lives are not comparable to those of older women. In my survey results, older people seem better off.

As was seen above, after the "honeymoon period" culture shock becomes intense but then diminishes. Question two asks respondents how long they have been in the United States so far. The hypothesis is that after the first six months to twelve months in the United States, the wives will experience less culture shock as they master the language and understand American rules and customs better.

Respondents indicate that they have lived from two months to forty-one months in the United States. Fourteen are in the high culture shock period. One had only two months' experience, two for four months, three for eight months, three for ten months, two for eleven months and three for twelve months. The rest had lived in the period of diminishing culture shock after one year. Six had stayed for sixteen months, two for eighteen months and two for twenty-two months. Despite differences in time spent in the United States, all respondents indicate similar levels of culture shock. Of course, some people who are in the United States longer are having an easier time in daily life including simple English conversation. I suspect that almost all respondents no matter how long they have been in the United States are so involved in taking care of their children or protecting them that they have no time for themselves. Their family duties may be stopping them from learning about a new culture.

Culture shock diminishes when people have previous intercultural experiences. Question three asks whether or not they had visited the United States before. Nine respondents reply that they had come to the United States before; six of them on their honeymoons when they would not be learning about the local culture. One traveled to Hawaii for two weeks. Two others had lived in Los Angeles before for two or three years. The latter two indicated that they were better prepared to come but also claimed that Tennessee differs from the West Coast.

In Question four respondents indicate if they have visited other countries too. My hypothesis is that people who have visited other countries also would have less culture shock because they have been through it before even if they never visited the United States.

Fourteen respondents had visited other countries for an average of two weeks, usually for sightseeing or honeymoons. I strongly suspect that they used packaged tours and had interpreters, so they never confronted the local culture alone. Only one person answers that the purpose of her visit was to study a language and to travel. She stayed two months, the longest in the sample. Although she has been in the United States for about eleven months so far, she says she has had no homesickness.

Alternatively, in Question five, I ask respondents whether they had ever moved to a different city before. The reason for asking this question is that people who have experienced moving may have less stress in their new environments. These people should also be more active in making new friends, adjusting to new things or learning about new areas.

In the responses only two people moved to other cities which I could consider might have different customs. These were not differences that could demonstrate the hypothesis.

If personality type affects the experience of culture shock, Question six is designed to test the hypothesis. Respondents make self-assessments of their personalities as very positive, positive, in between, negative or very negative.

Half the respondents rated themselves in between, a normal Japanese tendency. Only one said very positive, thirteen were positive, and only five were negative. Because Japanese wish to appear in the middle, I did not receive sincere self-assessments that would demonstrate a relationship to culture shock.

Expectations are also important in minimizing culture shock. Question seven asks respondents what they thought when notified they were coming to live in the United States.

Most respondents were not unhappy to come but worried about many things. Only one-quarter of the respondents said they were pleased to come. A few respondents mentioned that they would be more free of obligations in the United States. Only two were unhappy about the trip, usually because they had to leave parents and friends. The major worry was about their children's health and education. Almost all respondents mentioned the demands of the Japanese educational system when their children return. Besides children, they worried about speaking English, the food, sickness, housing, leaving things in Japan, and condition of old parents and relatives. Many also worried about their husband's job and health. I found that the women did not worry about taking care of themselves but about their children and husbands. The experience of culture shock would come indirectly through its effects on others.

Question eight asks respondents about their expectations for themselves on coming to the United States. The hypothesis is that those who had expectations to learn or do something new would experience less culture shock and get over it faster.

The majority wished to improve their English conversation skills. Others wished to travel or learn skills, such as quilting. Four of them mentioned they expect they could meet Americans and become friends. A few planned to escape relations with family or neighbors. Looking at all the responses, I have the impression that many are not trying hard to adjust to American culture knowing that they are returning to Japan in a couple of years.

Experiences of Culture Shock

The second section of the questionnaire elicits experiences of culture shock. In question nine I ask about frequency and form of homesickness. My hypothesis is that wives experience homesickness, just as students do.

The majority answered that they get homesick, while sixteen of the thirty-five claimed they do not. As expected, some people are frequently homesick at first, but later get better. One said that she gets homesick before or after the wife-association meetings. Another said she gets homesick whenever she confronts a problem. Many said that feel they want to go back to Japan to see parents, siblings, relatives, friends or pets. One said she wants to let her grandparents hug her children and to watch Japanese TV Another said she feels nothing but emptiness, so she does not want to talk to anyone except family. Still another says she does not want to go back but does not want to be here either. Clearly some are experiencing intense homesickness. Those who deny it may also be covering it up.

Finally, I ask how the respondents deal with their homesickness when they have it. Many write letters or call their families. Others visit Japanese friends. They also shop, play sports or amuse themselves. A few eat a lot of food, read books or grumble at their Japanese friends or husbands. Coping strategies are talking to their husband or ignoring the housework.

Successful adjustment to culture shock leads to personal growth. In question ten I ask whether or not they have changed in the United States. I want to compare the responses with those of university students.

Eleven respondents claimed they had not changed. I wonder how hard these people are trying to adjust themselves to a new environment. Ten others felt good changes in themselves. Becoming more open-minded, strong or cheerful were common answers. One said she became very direct in stating her ideas. Another said she felt released from worrying about fashions. One lady mentioned that she became more understanding about her husband and his work. Another found she could look at Japan and the United States more fairly. Others had negative experiences. Many mentioned that they were nervous, careful about small matters, concerned about how others viewed them, and mentally tired. A few started to scold their children more often, especially about their studies. Some had difficulties keeping in harmony with other Japanese. Another avoids activities that the company is involved in.

In contrast in a study of Japanese women students in the same city a year earlier:

> All of the participants felt they had been changed by their experiences abroad. The Japanese women all said they felt stronger and more assertive because of their experiences in America. One said her experiences have changed her from a "typical Japanese shy girl to a typical American wild girl." (Huffman, p.19)

Clearly Japanese women college students respond that they are strongly influenced by American culture and participate enthusiastically in it, while housewives maintain their separation from American culture.

Culture shock also affects relationships with one's family. The husband's help can make the culture shock much less. In question eleven I ask the respondents about changes in their relationships and what would their husbands do if they experience difficulties.

Four-fifths of the wives answered that their relationship with their husband has not changed after coming to America. Six said their relationships got better or much better. One said it was worse.

Most answered that their husbands listen to them very well but that is all. Usually they leave to her matters concerning the children, the home interior, and the wife's social life. Some complain that their husbands do not have time to help because they come home so late. I had some answers that wives try not to ask their husband for help because their husbands are too busy. This attitude is very common in Japan.

It was very disappointing to me that most of the respondents' relationships have not changed. They see many American couples helping each other, talking to each other, and caring about time spent together.

How then do Japanese women fill their time in the United States? Question twelve tests the hypothesis that most respondents do not have time to do something for themselves. The traditional way of thinking in Japan assumes that having fun as a couple means to sacrifice one's children. If they did, though, they could relieve their own stress.

Most answered that child-rearing takes up their time. Many complained about taking children to school, friends' houses, and private lessons, especially those with more than one child. Checking homework and children's home study in Japanese are major efforts. Household chores consume all day, since husbands here can come home for lunch.

One gave a very interesting answer. A senior wife said most of her time taking care of other wives in the company. It is not unusual for older people to take care of younger people in Japan, so her answer seems very natural, although it also depends on her personality.

Question thirteen asks about the use of free time. Twenty-nine said they had some free time. Some wives spend time for hobbies, friends or volunteer work. Those who said they had no time have small children. They feel they must stay with them all day long because they would feel guilty putting their children in day care. This way of thinking is very common in Japan.

The "sour stage" of culture shock leads to preoccupation with worries and inconveniences. In question fourteen I ask what these are. Most answered they were concerned about their children's school education after they return to Japan. I can say that children's education is a major concern of all Japanese mothers.

Some are concerned about family members' health. Their husbands work hard and might get sick. One was afraid she would get sick too. Another has a chronic ailment and fears it will worsen here. Others worry about parents and children remaining in Japan. One worried about her dear dog back in Japan.

One woman finds no good friend to talk to, while another worries because too many other Japanese families live in her neighborhood, so she has to worry about having good relationships with them.

Several mentioned the lack of public transportation in America. They have to transport the children themselves.

Others could not find good Japanese food or ingredients. They needed help with English and were frustrated that they could not communicate.

At the "enjoyment stage" after culture shock respondents appreciate parts of the culture and intentionally avoid irritating parts. If they are stuck in the "sour stage" the irritating parts remain at the forefront. However, for Japanese raised to be polite, the questions themselves, "What do you like?" and "What do you hate?," provoke culture shock.

On the question "What do you like?" they appreciated cheerful, openhearted and nice American people, big houses with extensive gardens, and the rich nature with many kinds of animals. Some said they liked freedom in American life. For instance, one woman lived with her husband's parents in Japan and had to be sensitive about everything, but now she does not have to be that way. Another said she has no troublesome people in her present life.

As for "What do you hate?" they mentioned inability to communicate in English, lack of fresh seafood and Japanese food, inconvenience without public transportation, and mowing grass.

Some mentioned being uncomfortable as Japanese in America. One said that she feels discrimination as an Oriental. Another mentioned she became aware of how Japanese she is and how she prefers Japanese surroundings.

Three women commented that they do not like associating with other Japanese people. One woman said that the company wives' association was too nosy. Another said there are troubles and struggles among Japanese people here. Still another says she dislikes associating with other Japanese people. These three have adapted enough to American culture to prefer its individualism.

Another question asks "What are you surprised at?" Some answers were many churches, simple cooking, big houses, cheap living costs, expensive medical care, and new ways to care for the family.

Some surprises represent culture shock. Several found that restaurants serve large portions of food and drinks and that people are fat. The roads are so big and wide and people drive broken-down cars. One woman was surprised that Americans put their children in day-care so they can both work. Another was horrified that her English teacher chews on candies and gum during class. They also find it strange that old people drive alone. Many of them are surprised at the independence of women and the elderly in America.

As for the question "What are you disappointed with?" many complain about food. American cooking is either too sweet, too salty or too sour. Americans miss appointments and break promises. They stare at Japanese and are ignorant about Japan. All of these responses represent culture shock.

A few women mentioned that they were disappointed to have to associate so much with Japanese. One commented that "association with Japanese is treacherous."

The responses to the above questions parallel those for Japanese women students, who also missed Japanese food, marveled at the open landscapes, and found the transportation system peculiar (Huffman, p.19). Students who overcome culture shock also try to distance themselves from associations of Japanese.

Question eighteen asks how first impressions of the United States have changed. My hypothesis is that if the first impressions change for the better, then the person is overcoming culture shock.

Many arrived with the belief that the United States is a very dangerous place to live. They relaxed when they discovered that Tennessee is not like New York City. They also discovered that American people are kind and friendly.

Others' first impressions turned to disappointment. The complaints were all different. The underlying cause was often poor English speaking skill.

Efforts to Cope with Culture Shock

This last section examines respondents' own efforts to overcome culture shock. These efforts include intentionally meeting American people, taking English conversation lessons, etc.

Question sixteen asks how much they associate with other Japanese. People who only associate with their own group do not adjust to the new culture quickly. They would have serious culture shock too.

One-fifth of the respondents answered they were associating with other Japanese on purpose. Five-sevenths said they did not know why they associated with other Japanese. Most did so to let their children play together or to have someone to talk to. One woman said, "I want to associate with both Japanese and Americans more freely, but because of my English skill, I tend to associate with Japanese [more] than Americans. It is easier that way." Though they wish to associate with Americans, it is easier not to.

In question seventeen, they indicate how much they associate with American people and where they meet them. Meeting Americans would help them learn language, customs or rules quickly, so they have less difficulties in the new culture.

Only two-fifths said they were deliberately trying to associate with American people. The rest did not know. Typical responses were: "I just greet them"; "I met them through my children"; "When our private lesson teachers come"; "We spend two to three hours with a host family"; "When I am invited, I invite them back." The places where they usually meet American people are their neighborhoods, children's schools, their own teachers or wives of American company wives. Two women had more purposeful ways to meet Americans. One woman found she met Americans through participation in a country club where her children play sports. Another said she made many friends through her host family.

Two questions ask about language learning. Question eighteen asks about kinds of formal lessons and nineteen asks about other ways to improve language ability through use of TV, tapes, radio or talking with Americans. My hypothesis is that people who are good at English have less difficulty with conversation and can actively learn the new culture.

One-quarter did not study English. One of them was afraid of being ashamed in front of everyone. Another felt she is too old to learn the language. Another finds no need because her husband and children will speak English for her. The others took expensive individual lessons rather than classes. The fear of making mistakes in English prevented them from taking classes with college students.

Many women watch TV or read the newspapers to improve their English, though they cannot understand much. Others try to listen to radio or tapes. One person sent to Japan for English materials. Four women said they did nothing and three did not answer. Generally they are not using the mass media purposefully to learn English. They even answer the phone in Japanese. When I asked some why they did not say, "Hello," they replied they were afraid of having to talk more. I think that they can practice English in situations like this.

Their attitude is summarized in responses to a question: "Do you think that you are really trying to associate with American people?" Half said, "No." The main reason was poor English speaking skill or feeling tired trying to speak to Americans in English. A few said they think the language problem may bother American people. This is clear evidence of culture shock.

Question twenty-two asks if they want the College to provide more programs for them. I noticed that quite a lot wanted the College to give them opportunities to get to know Americans. Two women mentioned wanting to know how to order in restaurants, how to identify kinds of flowers and plants in America, how to take care of a car, or how to consult a doctor. They need lessons in functional English.

I also ask if there is any constraint or impediment to doing what they wish. I believe that many women have unusual hobbies or special skills they could offer.

The majority answered, "Yes." Many people mentioned the language problem as the reason. Some wives resist putting their children in day care to pursue their own hobbies. One said she wished to, but her husband disagrees. Five others said other Japanese wives prevented them from doing so. As one said, "The nosiness of Japanese wives in the same company is becoming a great pressure on me, but I am trying to do what I want to do." Another mentioned that doing anything very different can bring blame from other wives.

Part of the limitation on their contact with American culture may be imposed by authority figures: their husband, the company or bosses' wives. Question twenty-five asks about the need to get permission for leaving town, taking or giving lessons, having a baby sitter, going golfing or to a health club, and organizing a party.

While most answered that they need their husband's permission for everything on the list, I interpret that as informing their husband about activities. The company's permission is needed for them to go to Atlanta, leave on a family trip or teach a class. Only a few indicated that they need permission from bosses' wives for going to Atlanta, organizing a party, leaving on a family trip, or letting their children do something different than other Japanese children. I am suspicious about these answers, since many have mentioned to me how intrusive the company and the bosses' wives are in their lives.

Culture shock may be reduced through preparation. Question twenty-six asks for advice to Japanese wives who will come in the future.

Many respondents stated the need for English conversational ability before departure from Japan. Some indicated the need to bring a hobby or objects to share with people here, both Americans and other Japanese. Some also wished to reassure future wives who are nervous about coming. They recommended going out and becoming very active. A few noted difficulties in maintaining harmony among Japanese women. I would summarize the responses as advising Japanese wives coming in the future to have better English speaking skills, strong personalities, willingness to adjust to new culture, and much more realistic information about life here.

Finally, I ask for further comments in the questionnaire. Several were very revealing. A woman reported that she was confused by company policy. Is it Japanese style or American style? Another woman often feels she is living in an illusion, like she is still in Japan. A different woman mentioned the strange feeling of seeing a group of Japanese people talking in Japanese in America. Some said they felt closer now to their native land, Japan. All of these responses indicate culture shock.

Many requested copies of the results of the survey. Some also encouraged me to continue. Their comments made me happy that I chose to study culture shock.

RECOMMENDATIONS

I would like to provide background on the above responses before giving my own recommendations. The majority of the Japanese wives did not want to come to the United States to live. Even among those who were neutral about coming, their reasons were to escape from constraints in Japan. While their living is comfortable, they are highly restricted by their husbands, companies, or bosses' wives with all kinds of rules. The company wants American people to look at them as model families. For example, a husband tells his wife not to drive to another city because too many accidents occur on the highway. He is afraid that an accident will happen to her and damage the company's image. Another example is that the company tells mothers of small children to control them in the shopping mall without scolding them in public. Younger wives complain that bosses' wives are mean and demanding about too many things. They must follow all kinds of rules or customs exactly as in Japan. They brought "Japanese society" with its rules and customs to the United States.

By recreating Japanese society, they reduce culture shock. The wives are not aware of culture shock because in a sense they never left Japanese culture. At the same time they feel more difficulty in approaching American culture.

To help them adjust I would give them this advice:

- Wipe out the idea that you did not want to come. Forget you only have a little time before returning. Even nowadays not many Japanese have the opportunity to live outside their own culture. Living in America is an experience to be appreciated to its fullest.
- Take every opportunity to speak English with neighbors, in stores, answering the phone, closed-captioned TV. Practice systematically, prepare vocabulary, and discuss progress with Americans afterwards.
- Do not be afraid to ask Americans for help. Asking people for help is not a source of shame.
- Use baby-sitters and daycare in order to have time for yourself and your husband.
- Do not stick to "Japanese society" so much if you want to enjoy your stay in America.

CONCLUSION

Culture shock is a problem for companies preparing to send families overseas. It can cause personal pain, alienate foreigners and also reduce the efficiency of business people. Several methods exist for minimizing culture shock. A company responsible for sending personnel overseas should:

(1) screen employees and families carefully to avoid incipient physical or mental problems,
(2) choose those with previous experience not only in business but also in adapting to foreign cultures,
(3) support their sense of identity while encouraging them to explore the foreign culture, and
(4) provide opportunities for preparation before travel.

At the same time the families must make an effort

(1) to see value in this experience overseas,

(2) to learn the language and culture before and during their stay,
(3) to find time to share their marriage and family life, and
(4) to make opportunities to meet the people asking them for advice and help rather than asking other Japanese.

CULTURE SHOCK QUESTIONNAIRE*

1. Your age	2. Your husband's age
20-25 ______	20-25 ________
26-30 ______	26-30 ________
31-35 ______	31-35 ________
36-40 ______	36-40 ________
41-45 ______	41-45 ________
46-50 ______	46-50 ________
51-55 ______	51-56 ________
56+ ______	56+ ________

2. How long have been in the U.S. so far?
   about _____ months

3. Have you visited the U.S. before? Yes___ No___
   For those who answer "Yes" when__________ where_______
   What was the purpose? __________________

4. Have you visited other countries besides the U.S.? Yes__ No__
   For those who answer "Yes" when________ where_____________
   For how long _____________ What was the purpose?___________

5. When you were a child, did you experience moving to a different city, for example, because of your parents' jobs? Yes__ No__
   For those who answer "Yes" how many ________________________
   how many __________________________
   domestic or overseas? ____________for how long _________

---

* questionnaire translated from Japanese

6. For many kinds of events, you are:
   very positive ______
   positive ___________
   not positive or negative _________
   negative _________
   very negative ______

7. When you were notified about coming and living in the U.S. for the first time, what did you think about it? Were you happy? Did you just hate it? Please be specific.

8. Did you have any expectations for coming to the U.S. to stay?
   [i.e., learning English conversation, patchwork, making many American friends. . .anything]

9. Do you get homesick? Yes___ No___
   For those answering "Yes" How often do you get homesick? [i.e., once a month, almost always]

   What kinds of homesickness are they?
   [i.e., want to go back to Japan, just feel sad, want to eat native food. . . etc.] Please be specific.

   When you are homesick, how do you deal with it?
   [i.e., drinking alcohol, doing sports, eat, smoke cigarettes, doing shopping, call to Japan or write to Japan, visiting Japanese friends who are living here] Please be specific and write as many as you want.

10. Have you changed since you left Japan and came to the U.S.? If so, how have you changed? [i.e., depression, smoking and drinking increased, physical changes, nothing seems important, scolding children differently, becoming negative, feeling mentally weak, etc.] Please feel free to write as much as you want.

11. In daily life in the U.S., when you are in trouble, what does husband do? [i.e., totally depends on me, ignores me, tries to help me, etc.] Please be specific.
    Compared to before when you and your husband were in Japan, the relationship between you and your husband was:
    much better__ better__ unchanged__ worse__ much worse__

12. What do you spend time on most in your daily life?
    [i.e., for children, taking them somewhere, bringing them back, checking homework, associating with other Japanese wives, volunteer work, housework, etc.] Please be specific.

13. Do you have personal time to spend on yourself? Yes__ No__
    For those answering "Yes": How do you spend the time?
    For those answering "No": Why do you not have any?

14. What are you most worried about?
    What most inconveniences you in the U.S.?

15. In American life, what do you like?
    What do you hate?
    What are you surprised by?
    What are you disappointed about?

16. How often do you associate with other Japanese people now?
    Associating with Japanese is something I do purposefully?
    Something that happens? Do not know?

17. How often do you associate with American people?
    Associating with Americans is something I do purposefully?
    Something that happens? Do not know?
    Where do you usually meet Americans? [i.e., at church, at children's sporting events, etc.]

18. What was your first impression about the U.S. and American people?
    How has it changed now?

19. Did you take any English lessons before you came to the U.S.?
    Yes__ No__
    For those answering "Yes" how often? Times per week___
    Length of lessons___ Number of months___
    For those answering "No" why not?

20. Are you taking any English lessons now? Yes__ No__
    For those answering "Yes" how often? Times per week__
    Length of lessons___ Where? From whom?
    For those answering "No" why not?

21. What are you trying to do in order to improve your English skill?
    [i.e., watching TV, listening to tapes or radio,
    associating a lot with Americans]

22. Do you have any requests to Maryville College to help besides English lessons? [i.e., culture series, field trips, shopping, etc.] Please feel free to request several.

23. Although this question covers part of Question 17, do you think that you are really trying to associate with Americans? Yes__ No__
    For those answering "No" is there any reason for not actively associating with Americans? [i.e., poor language skill, dislike Americans, worry about discord with other Japanese, etc.]

24. Suppose you have something that you want to do. Is there any impediment in to doing it? Or, do you have such feelings?
    Yes__ No__
    For those answering "Yes" what is the reason? [i.e., husband, company, bosses' wives, disagreements, pressure] Please feel free to write specifically.

25. Please indicate if you need permission and from whom for each of the following:

	Husband	Company	Bosses' wives
Going to Knoxville			
Going to Atlanta			
Taking lessons			

Hiring a baby sitter
Having a party with Americans
Having a party with Japanese
Going on a family trip
Teaching a course, like flower arrangement
Letting children do something different from other Japanese
Going to a health club
Associating with American people
Going golfing
Other__________

26. Please feel free to write any advice to Japanese wives who are coming to the U.S. in the future.

27. Please feel free to write any comments, advice, or opinions on this questionnaire.

Thank you for your cooperation

REFERENCES

M.S. Bassis, R.J. Gelles, and A. Levine *Sociology: AnIntroduction* New York: Random House, 1988.

L. Copeland and L. Griggs (Eds.) *Going International: How to make Friends and deal effectively in the Global Marketplace* New York: Random House, 1985.

S. Fisher *Homesickness, Cognition and Health* East Sussex, U.K.: Lawrence Erlbaum, 1989.

A. Furnham and S. Bochner (Eds.) *Culture Shock: Psychological Reactions to Unfamiliar Environments* New York: Routledge, 1989.

E.A. Hartung *Difficulties in Cultural Adjustment and Implications for Orientation of Japanese High-school Students Living in America* Unpublished master's thesis, University of California, Los Angeles, CA, 1983.

H. Huffman *Culture Shock: Its Analysis, Stages, and Results* Unpublished senior thesis, Maryville College, Maryville, TN, 1990.

Hur, Sonja Vegdahl and Ben Seunghwa Hur *Culture Shock! Korea* Singapore: Singapore Times Book International, 1988.

Oberg, K. "Culture Shock and the Problem of Adjustment in New Cultural Environments." In E.C. Smith and L.F. Luce (Eds.), *Toward Internationalism* (pp.43-45). Rowley, MA: Newbury House.

Conclusion

THE IMPACT OF JAPANESE INVESTMENT

Scott Brunger and Young-Bae Kim

In previous chapters the conclusions give a number of practical suggestions for managers of international companies and leaders in American communities. These suggestions include modifications of Japanese personnel management for American workers, adaptations of machinery and American work habits to minimize cumulative trauma injuries in the workplace, recognition of the many sources of support for foreign investment in an American community, and preparation of Japanese families for culture shock in America.

The underlying theme of this book is the cross-cultural influence of foreign investment. This cross-cultural influence goes both ways. The obvious direction of influence is the foreign firm bringing its corporate culture into the host community. The counter-flow of influence is not so obvious but just as necessary if the corporation is going to benefit from globalization, as discussed in the Introduction. While most people perceive a purposeful foreign firm impacting a passive community, the previous chapters indicate that the impacts have gone both ways.

Japanese firms have trained American managers and workers in their methods of work, holding Americans to the same productivity and quality standards as in Japan. In Chapter Two, Larry Thomas gives an example of the success of a Japanese firm in maintaining its standards in a U.S. joint venture. In Chapter Three, Brunger and Kim show that another Japanese firm has far-ranging economic effects through increasing the earning power of American workers and managers, expanding the tax base, providing new markets for selected local suppliers, and introducing a Japanese clientele as a distinct market niche for local merchants. These positive effects create goodwill that induces other Japanese firms to follow.

As previous chapters also show, this process has not been one-way. In Chapter One, Noriko Chapman discusses how Japanese management must treat women workers better than in Japan. Her example in obtaining a Masters in Business Administration shows that she expects the same changes to take place in personnel management in Japan too. Chapter Two gives examples of machinery modifications designed to eliminate situations where human handling of parts might result in injury. These modifications were useful enough that they were transferred back to Japan and implemented to save labor there. In Chapter Four, Manami Miura shows that Japanese business wives learn from their experience in the United States too. Their children who attend American schools become very acculturated into America and face the problems that all expatriate children do. They become experienced in three cultures: Japanese culture, American culture, and the culture created by expatriates who do not feel at home in the other two. The Japanese companies are changing through their experience in America.

This conclusion that Japanese firms have been changed should not surprise anyone familiar with Japanese management theory. After all it developed out of a marriage between the American Edward Deming's quality control techniques and Japanese culture. Japanese management brought to America already is a successful hybrid. Now this process of cross-cultural fertilization is continuing.

The idea of cross-cultural influence might serve as a research agenda for analyzing foreign investment in other communities too. The maps in the text above indicate locations of Japanese vehicle assembly plants in the United States and autoparts plants in East Tennessee, where similar cross-cultural influences can be expected. In addition, the German firms BMW built a new motor vehicle complex in Greeneville and Spartanburg in South Carolina where other German firms are already implanted and Mercedes constructed a plant outside Birmingham, Alabama near I-65.

A new source of cross-cultural influence comes in the North American Free Trade Agreement. Already free trade with Canada since 1988 has resulted in major relocations of vehicle assembly and auto-parts plants as manufacturers responded to increased international competition by eliminating duplicate plants. The net effect of the relocations has favored the United States, which is to be expected since Canadian motor vehicle production at 2.3 million units in 1994 is small compared to U.S. production at 12.3 million units. In the short run, the inclusion of Mexico in the North American vehicle market is likely to have minimal effects since the Mexican market is only 1.1 million units in 1994 (World

Almanac, p.212). Since assembly plants are most likely to gravitate toward the center of the North American auto industry located between Interstate I-65 and I-75 near Fort Wayne, Indiana, the inclusion of Canada and Mexico does not alter their optimal location. However, in the long run U.S. and Canadian demand for autos will grow slowly while the Mexican auto market should expand rapidly as Mexicans reach a standard of living that supports private cars. Eventually the growing Mexican market would shift the center of the auto industry southwards towards Tennessee.

In addition, some autoparts production which is labor intensive and inexpensive to transport will move to Mexico. Rubenstein lists assembly work on wiring, electronic components, trim, seat covers, belts, and bumpers (p.244). The technically more demanding stages of production of autoparts and bulky parts that are close to final assembly will be produced near vehicle assembly plants according to the system of just-in-time delivery. Fortunately for East Tennessee, factories specialized in steering systems, dashboard assemblies, and air-conditioning controls fall in the categories likely to remain in the United States, though some components may be imported from Mexico in the future. The auto industry is likely to remain an important part of local manufacturing in East Tennessee.

REFERENCES

Rubenstein, James *The Changing U.S. Auto Industry: A Geographical Analysis* London: Routledge, 1992.

The World Almanac and Book of Facts 1996 Mahwah, N.J.:Funk & Wagnalls Corp.

INDEX

D

E

F

G

H

I

J

K

L

M

N

O

P

Q

R

S

T

U

V

W